GET FOCUSED!
HOW TO ABIDE IN JESUS CHRIST

JOSEPH PAUL CRUM

ISBN 978-1-63874-387-3 (paperback)
ISBN 978-1-63874-388-0 (digital)

Christian Faith Publishing, Inc.
832 Park Avenue
Meadville, PA 16335
www.christianfaithpublishing.com

Printed in the United States of America

CONTENTS

PREFACE

Writing this book was fun. I wrote it with care for Christians. Not those people who claim to believe in God, but for those who know Him. After five years of calling myself a Christian, I was born new in faith through Jesus Christ. It happened while I was a sniper team leader in the US Army. Then I went to war.

Since returning from Afghanistan, I have wrestled with God and lost. There has been another war from the beginning that never ends. I'm talking about the battle of living a worthy life as a faithful follower of Jesus Christ. The mission God has given us is to follow Him and to teach others how to do the same. Studying the Bible, praying throughout each day, and staying plugged in with other believers has helped me grow in my walk with Christ. The Department of Veterans Affairs (VA) even put me through an undergrad degree, as well as a master of divinity. Still, I have lost focus when pulled to the left and the right along the way.

During the second lockdown for COVID-19 in 2020, I completed the Behavioral Financial Advisor designation to help guide others in making better financial decisions in line with what is most important to them. The concept involves identifying the top values that direct your ideal behavior. Some refer to this as values-aligned or values-based decision-making.

Values-aligned behavior is a proven strategy in psychology to behave more consistently in line with how one claims one ought to behave. It has infiltrated business and personal growth for individuals as well as organizations. The values-based approach to making financial decisions resonated with me because of my values-aligned focus in my own life, especially in my walk with Jesus. More important than having a financial plan is to use everything I possess to live a worthy life for God's glory. The concept comes not from psychology, nor the business world, but the Bible.

Because psychology fails to address sin and spiritual powers (such as demonic beings), I believe that the Bible is the only logical starting point for anyone wanting to live differently. Using a values-based approach to what the Bible has to say about how to live, I now have a road map for my entire life until the Lord calls me home or He returns.

Systematic theology involves studying what the entire Bible has to say about a topic, such as stewardship. The ultimate purpose of systematic theology and all study of God in the Bible for me is for practical application in my everyday life. The knowledge of God given to us in Scripture is practical for our personal lives. I am a student of the Bible in this way. Studying Paul's writings apart from James, Peter, John, Jonah, Moses, David, and any other biblical author does not make sense when the goal is to apply God's Word to how one should live. God chose all of those men to be His messengers for our benefit. Their words have authority over the follower of Jesus Christ. My respect for Scripture's authority shaped this book. However, this is not a work of systematic theology. It is more of a personal manifesto for leadership as a disciple-maker.

The call of God is a life of submission to the work He is doing in you and me. Submission is not always something that comes easy. A values-based approach to living how I believe the Bible teaches that I should live helped me get focused.

My prayer for you is that this book encourages you to be a good steward of everything God gives you and to live more purposefully in your calling in Jesus Christ as a result. Know Him more and more as you make Him known!

GET FOCUSED

GET FOCUSED

Have you ever been in the right place at the right time? I'm talking about one of those moments where you had an epiphany, knowing that you were in the exact time and place where you were supposed to be.

Ever since I was about four years old, the only thing I ever wanted to do was to get paid to rappel out of helicopters and sneak around the jungle. No other job ever appealed to me, and it seemed unavoidable.

On the morning of September 11, 2001, I was sitting on my duffel bags in Fort Benning, Georgia, waiting to start my first day of basic training. Despite the chaos that filled the next few days (9/11 postponed my training a few weeks), I had peace about being where God wanted me to be.

By the time I left for Afghanistan in 2004, I felt like the right man for the job. My job was to collect and report valuable battlefield information, sort of like being the eyes and ears of people who make big decisions. All the training for the worst-case scenario paid off. Plus, it was amazing to experience a steadfast faith and trust in God during that first year in Afghanistan.

The honeymoon phase of effortless trust in God ended after returning home to Hawaii in 2005, as all honeymoons do. There certainly seemed to be a wilderness-wandering season in my life after the Lord called me to follow Him. The call on my life for pastoral leadership was clear while in Afghanistan from 2004 to 2005. However, after more than four years overseas as a sniper team leader and in diplomatic security, I had broken relationships, and my life was a train wreck.

Transitioning from the military can be difficult for some people. It has been difficult for me. I felt like the right guy to be a sniper team leader in combat. There was an unspoken expectation of being the most dependable, most reliable guy in the world, yet it felt effortless at the time. It was like winning the Super Bowl and World Series in the same year. After that, what does a person do with their life?

Oh, this is not about the military. My transition out of a military mind-set has indeed proven to be complicated. I'm talking about my life before Christ and the war of submission after He called me to follow Him. When God called me to Himself for salvation through Jesus, I was on fire to tell everyone about Him. Coming to know my eternal destiny with God is guaranteed by His Spirit gave me great comfort. However, overconfidence based on previous experiences has led to disappointment along the way. Expectations can ruin our day if we do not view life through the lens of Christ. Chasing after things of the world rather than a relationship with my heavenly Father has also disappointed me. It has been a painful transition. Yeah, submission is a tricky thing when pride is your most significant character defect. Pride keeps us from abiding in Christ. To say it another way, pride keeps us from being faithful to Him.

Have you ever considered what it was like for the Israelites to come out of Egypt? Finally, free of bondage through the incredible miracles of God on their behalf. It seems so unreal that they would then turn around and build an altar to a false god to worship. And you know that every human being on the planet who has come to trust in Jesus Christ as their Savior and Great King is guilty of doing the same thing. Kind of like my poor choices after experiencing freedom from sin through the gospel and having unforgettable experiences of God's protection while in combat. Why did they doubt God and keep looking back to Egypt after seeing His miraculous deliverance from slavery? (Again, this is about pride and my lack of trust in God's faithfulness.)

It was not until a friend, Dr. Gary Ewen, invited me to a Values-Aligned Leadership Conference (VALS) in 2018 that I had that feeling of being in the right place at the right time again. At the conference, there was an emphasis on the importance of identifying personal core values. That night, I struggled to think of any values vital to me. Then, like a light bulb went off above my head, I remembered the army values from my time in basic training. The army values were easy to remember because the values formed the acronym **LDRSHIP**. Although they were not my core values, they did help spark something inside of me.

US Army Core Values
LDRSHIP

- Loyalty
- Duty
- Respect
- Selfless Service
- Honor
- Integrity
- Personal Courage

THE NUMBER 1 TOP VALUE

Years passed without thinking of the army values, yet they all came to mind instantly as soon as I thought of that acronym LDRSHIP. That is the brilliance of poetic devices. Those are some great values for a soldier, but they were not central to whom I had become. As I began praying about what is most important to me, one word kept popping out: *stewardship*.

My uncle, Tommy, could not walk or talk (he had cerebral palsy). I was three or four years old when I asked my mom why he couldn't do what the rest of us could do. She explained that not everyone could do those things. Additionally, she let me know that it was essential to make good use of my abilities. Whether she knew it or not, my mother instilled a philosophy of stewardship with her thoughtful response. Her words impacted me. I'm grateful for them. Yet, so often, regardless of my accomplishments, I have felt guilty for not doing more with the gifts and abilities God has given me.

Have you ever been paralyzed emotionally from feeling like a failure in life? That has certainly been part of my story. There are no examples that come to mind when I felt that way in combat. Not for a second. Responding to explosions and gunfights felt like the days of stealing home on the pitch during a city league All-Star game. My first year in Afghanistan felt like being the MVP of the Major League All-Star game, not because I was the best but because God put me in the right places at the right time. It was unexplainable. My identity as a child of God and representative of His kingdom aligned with the discipline I had to be all I could be (old army slogan for those who remember). However, before combat and a few times afterward, I must admit that my poor decisions have hurt people close to me. How do you cope with the guilt of letting other people down? The fact that there are no time machines is a bummer.

Some people suffer from believing that they must do things perfectly. Nobody is perfect, yet there seems to be no escape from the relentless pursuit of perfection for some people. Pursuing excellence is a great thing. Without the discipline to practice flawless musical pieces, none of us would enjoy the beautiful sounds that move us emotionally. Being a perfectionist, on the other hand, can have devastating consequences. Discipline to do what is right also demands mercy.

My high school athletic career was less than impressive because substance abuse became more important than sports. Substances can end up becoming more important than people. At some point, substance abuse destroys every human relationship. A choice must be made to leave the abusive relationship with substances. Thankfully, God made that choice for me in 1998 when I crashed through private property after drinking a potentially lethal amount of alcohol and decided to drive very fast in my mom's minivan. (Sorry, Mom!)

When police arrested me, I was sitting in the driver's seat of a totaled vehicle in Burnsville, Minnesota, sometime after midnight on a summer night. Before that arrest, however, something happened to me that is hard to explain. Looking at the carnage caused in a residential neighborhood by missing a fifteen-mile-per-hour turn, an epiphany struck me like a lightning bolt. It was a miracle to be alive (and a miracle that I did not kill anyone). It is scary to think about, but I realized I was driving a vehicle only seconds before impact. As I sat in a destroyed minivan, a confident knowledge that angels protected me (again, not sure how to explain that I knew that at the time) and certainty that God exists changed my perception of things. I cannot explain it any better than that. He had saved me from death, and I knew it. The epiphany I had was that the God of the universe is real, and He is getting my attention. A few minutes later, I was handcuffed in the back of a police car.

Following that car crash at age nineteen, I found myself doing some serious soul-searching in a detox facility. The waves of guilt I felt over squandering my natural abilities were like torture while stuck in that facility. Beating myself up physically as well as internally over poor decision-making did not accomplish anything. However, one night while everyone else was sleeping, a man came out to where I was sitting, lost in my thoughts, and he told me something that changed the trajectory of my guilt. The man said to me that he knew God was calling him to turn from his drinking and to get back on track with Jesus. Whoa!

How do you "get back on track with Jesus" when you feel lost and like a failure? How do you get on the track in the first place? It certainly helps to know that all the things you feel like God could never forgive are precisely the things that caused Jesus Christ to enter the broken world and go to the cross of crucifixion on your behalf. All the minor imperfections, those little sins that we are guilty of, are included, but it hits us at the core to know that our Father in heaven proved His great love for us by sending Jesus to pay for our selfish mistakes. It helps to know that He has a purpose for us to make good use of everything He gives.

After being born from above in Christ, poor decision-making did not disappear overnight. Stewardship of the natural abilities and time God has given me for developing genuine relationships has haunted me at times due to my shortcomings. Praise God that He forgives us in Christ and cleanses us from the stains of our guilt. Now, stewardship means to involve God in everything I do.

This book is about the importance of *stewardship* for the individual Christian and the global body of Christ. It is not possible to be a good steward of what God has entrusted while failing to remain in ongoing fellowship with Him. Notice that we will be viewing ideas about God and how we should live through defining and unpacking specific "values"—those things that are most important to us regarding our beliefs and behavior.

Values-based decision-making is about living a disciplined life and is not a new concept. God gave us an entire list of values that all followers of Jesus Christ are encouraged to excel in (2 Peter 1:5–8), along with several other lists. These happen to be the values for my life and walk with Christ. They do not make me more spiritual or a better person, but they help me focus on what is most important to me as a follower of Jesus Christ. These values, which I have defined through the lens of Scripture, help me to love God and love people. My hope is that it helps you to get focused on what is most important to you.

The power of God working in us (His Spirit) provides everything we need to live worthy lives of our calling as brothers and sisters in Jesus Christ. Identifying top personal core values has helped me get back to living with the discipline I once enjoyed as a sniper team leader. My top values provide greater consistency and precision in my daily life with God and other people. Stewardship, in my opinion, means involving God in everything. Not coincidentally, the things that are most important to me form the acronym STWRDSHIP:

Core Values for a Worthy Life
STeWaRDSHIP

- The Value of **S**implicity
- The Value of **T**hankfulness
- The Value of **W**isdom
- The Value of **R**epentance
- The Value of **D**iscernment
- The Value of **S**incerity
- The Value of **H**umility
- The Value of **I**nfluence
- The Value of **P**erseverance

While it is true that these are my core values that guide my desired behavior, you are free to use any or all of them. You are also free to create a list of those values which resonate deeply with you. I am passionate about stewardship, which might differ from your passion. We are on a journey to live with purpose, and I am grateful to be on the ride together.

Your mission is to get focused on following Jesus well and help others do the same. The only way to complete this mission is by remaining in an ongoing relationship with God. I'm talking about how to abide in Christ, and for me, it has everything to do with stewardship. It is the mission He has given to all Christians, which is why we will walk through unpacking stewardship as a core value in the following nine chapters. The end of each chapter provides a short exercise to reflect on for your own life. Included at the end of this book is a chapter for creating your own biblical values list, as well as a bonus chapter to make a quick plan to live more in line with your values. God created you for a purpose. I pray that you would know the joy and peace of God's purpose for your life in the mission He has given you until His return.

GOSPEL STEWARDSHIP

οἰκονομία, ας, ἡ
management of household affairs, **stewardship**,
administration

A man once had a vision. In this vision, every born-again follower of Jesus Christ, filled with the Spirit of God, used every gift, ability, and possession God had given for knowing the God of heaven and earth and living worthy lives as His image-bearers. His vision was of the kingdom of heaven, where there will never again be broken relationships.

This ideal reality became a passion and the sole focus of the man. He set out on a mission to encourage everyone he could find to be good stewards of everything God gives for the mission of knowing Him and making Him known. The man's passion was to do everything he could to help others experience a glimpse of this vision.

He soon found out that the passion God gave him would open people's eyes from all over the world. People from every religion and station in life began singing with joy in one city because of the man's shared vision. Still, the man learned quickly that more people opposed his message than those excited about it. His joy increased as more people became passionate about his vision, despite the growing hatred against him and the image of loving others eternally.

There were a few times that he felt almost hopeless. The man was attacked in public, beaten, and arrested multiple times. While sitting in prison, chained to a wall, he felt like he might be better off dead. Then, the vision God gave him provided strength. He sang with joy from his prison cell, causing every inmate and guard to wonder how anyone could have such peace and happiness. The guards and other prisoners thought he was a complete whack-a-doo.

Something interesting happened when the guards would ridicule the oddly joyful prisoner. His responses to them would change their attitude toward him. You see, he did not have all the answers, but he knew the Creator of the universe intimately, and they could tell. He prayed for them out loud. His explanations of how God entered the evil world to demonstrate His love toward evil people changed their minds. They began to think differently. The very people who mocked the man began living how they claimed a person should live. They believed the man, and they became passionate about the vision he shared.

It turns out that God's chosen messenger, Paul (also known as Saul), used the word *stewardship* to handle the message of salvation through faith in Christ (1 Corinthians 9:14–18). Wait, you might have missed that because it is too simple. Paul, the apostle, was a good steward of the good news of Jesus Christ. That is incredible! His goal was to make God known so that we would know God more and more.

As we continue to explore biblical stewardship, we learn that we are encouraged to be good stewards of everything God gives. According to another apostle, Peter, our purpose is to help others know God more. Peter said to use every word we speak and every action we do for God to be praised above all things forever (1 Peter 4:10–11). That is a high calling, for sure.

You'll never guess how Jesus used the word *stewardship*. Luke's gospel is the only record we have of Jesus ever using the word οἰκονομία, and it is worth studying (Luke 16:1–15). Okay, this will blow your mind, but Jesus told His listeners to use the wealth of the world—any possessions that can be deceptively used for evil—to make friends in this life. Our Lord did not just teach us to make friends with people, but friendships with eternal impact. Eternal relationships! That is the point of stewardship.

We are here on a mission to know God and to make Him known. The beauty of God's redemptive plan for humankind is that we have the freedom to pursue this mission with unique creativity. That is why using a values-based approach is how we are moving forward in the rest of the book to consider what it means to pursue a worthy life with greater focus.

> **Stewardship**: to use everything God gives for knowing Him more and making Him known in the world.

UNPACKING THE VALUE OF STeWARDSHIP

SIMPLICITY

Communicate clearly and concisely for life change

The unfolding of Your words gives light;
giving understanding to the simple.
—Psalm 119:130

Where were you when God began getting your attention? The first time I asked a man why his life was different than most people, the answer shocked me. At nineteen years old, I assumed that this gentleman nearing retirement would tell me that he got a good education, then a decent car, and a nice home, a wife; the kids followed along with rainbows and sunny days. There was nothing flashy about his lifestyle, far from it. But he had peace and joy in his face and his life.

Be ready to give a reason for the eternal hope that dwells inside you to those who ask. The moment of impact for me regarding Jesus was when I felt drawn to ask someone about his life. He had something I wanted in life, but I was not sure exactly what that *something* was. That means that I was ready to listen to the answer given to me.

The reason for this man's peace and joy was simple: Jesus. That is the answer I received. The exact response escapes me now, but it was something like, "Well, when I was a young man, I came to realize that I was a sinner in need of a savior, and I have been following Jesus ever since." That simple statement rocked my world. The answer was Jesus.

To kick off the unpacking of stewardship, we begin with the value of *simplicity*. Now, keeping things simple does not necessarily mean that it is easy to simplify. The message of the entire Bible is simple, but it certainly is not short.

Have you ever felt overwhelmed with the Bible? Having a better understanding of the message of the Bible is how my life has become more simplified. Therefore, that is where we begin.

There are a lot of pages and a lot of words in the Bible. God began getting my attention through a car crash. Not long after that, I tried to start reading in Genesis to learn about the God responsible for getting my attention without much success. It felt overwhelming.

My first mentor in the Christian faith, Milt Andrews, gave me my first Bible. Milt told me that the gospel of John is an excellent place to start for most people. That might not have resulted in much change then, but it helped to hear someone give a little guidance and got me to Jesus much more quickly than starting in Genesis.

Begin with Jesus

THE MESSAGE OF GOD TO HUMANKIND

How do we communicate the Old and New Testaments' entire contents to someone without saying too much and causing people's eyes to glaze over? Understanding the overall message of the Bible helps make sense out of every other aspect of life.

God began communicating to sinful people through chosen messengers. His purpose was to redeem fallen humankind from the effects of sin, which is the problem we are all born into in this life. The God we learn about in the Bible is highly relational, existing for eternity as Father, Son, and Spirit. His purpose in creating us is to extend His perfect, relational love to us so we can enjoy Him forever.

The Creator of heaven and earth calls us to make Him known to others so that more people can share in the eternal blessings given freely in Christ. That is the mission God has given us. Do you feel ill-equipped for the task? So did many people throughout the Bible. You and I are in good company. Consider that Jesus healed a man born blind. The man was no biblical scholar. When pressured about his healing, he spoke truthfully about the fact that Jesus healed him. It is that simple. Try it!

**I used to be blind but now I can see! Do
you want to follow Him, too?
—Dude who used to be blind answering the skeptics**

KNOW HIM

Do you believe in Jesus, or do you know Him? There is a question that can cause the deer-caught-in-the-headlights look.

A young college student met with me for coffee in Fort Collins, Colorado, to ask how to make sense of the Bible. He had recently come out of the occult, involved in dangerously prideful behavior and demonic thinking. As we began reading about Jesus in John's gospel, he fired off five questions before we made it through the first few verses. His questions were about why and how we could trust that anything in the Bible is true. I asked him if he believed that the sacrifice of Jesus Christ on the cross covers his sin so he can know God. He made it clear that he did not believe that Jesus was a sufficient Savior because he doubted the credibility of the Bible.

Dealing with an internal dilemma, he said that he needed more to go on than to "believe" that something is true. The compassion I felt for this man due to his visible struggle of faith led me to think about Milt Andrews's simple answer when I asked about his life. This guy did not ask me about my life. He just told me that he needed rescuing but now seemed to need answers about cosmic laws and philosophical reasoning. No answer I gave about the Bible slowed him from his next prepared question.

So, I said something that he was not expecting: "Look, I know you think that you need to believe in Jesus. The truth is that those demons you have been wrestling with also believe in Him and are terrified of Him. They are going to spend eternity apart from Him. I know Jesus, and it seems like He is getting your attention, so I agreed to meet with you today. Do you want to know Him too?"

When he heard that the point is not to believe in Jesus but to know Him, His eyes popped open a bit. He looked intrigued and was quiet for a few seconds. His face then dropped as though defeated. He asked me if I would pray for God to save him and that he had to go. For the next few minutes, I prayed for God to release him from the bondage of sin and demonic strongholds in his life. He never met up with me again. I do not even remember his name, but I pray for him to receive forgiveness and God's Holy Spirit when God brings the man to mind.

That day was insightful for me because getting to Jesus is the point. The meeting relieved some pressure to have all the answers because it caused me to become more focused. My mission is to know God more and make Him known. That is what I need to spend my time on.

Every human author whom God inspired to write Scripture through the centuries and across multiple continents wrote about the same thing. More specifically, they were all writing about the same Person. It is all about Jesus. He is the key to it all.

From the book of Genesis forward, there is an unfolding of revelation about Jesus. He is the Word, and the Light, giving under-standing to the simple. We either know Him, or we do not. We have either been crucified with Christ, and His Spirit dwells within us, or we do not belong to Him and remain dead in our sins. My goal is for you to know Him and for others to come to know Him through you.

> I am bound to preach Jesus Christ and Him
> crucified, for I do not know anything else to
> preach. My simplicity is my safeguard.
> —C. H. Spurgeon

THE REASON WE EXIST

People seem to become like those with whom they spend the most time. Maybe we need to be reminded once in a while that we need to spend time with Jesus.

The reason we are alive is simple. God has created us to enjoy Him and glorify Him forever. That is the highest purpose of humankind in the Westminster Catechism, summarizing the entire Bible's message. Many people sat down hundreds of years ago to study everything the Bible says about why we exist. Another group of faithful disciples did something similar, developing a document called the Heidelberg Catechism. All of this was in response to Christians not living how they should be living. These and many other faith statements came out of the diligent study of Scripture by people who did not have the distractions of television and smartphones. Instead, they took God at His word that He has given us everything we need for life and to be like Him (to glorify Him). Yet, there remains a tension to live how we ought to. You see it everywhere there are Christians.

How we are to live according to God in Scripture is simple. The primary issue is whether we are living how God has called us and commanded us to live. The whole Old Testament Law summarized is to love God and love people. Are we doing that?

THE SIMPLICITY OF THE BIBLE

The Old Testament pointed forward to Jesus, while the New Testament points back to Him. The New Testament points back to the Old Testament to point forward to Jesus. Both the Old and New Testaments point forward to His return, at which time every human being in history will spend eternity with or without God.

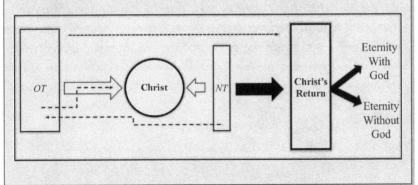

Through complete trust in Christ and by God's Holy Spirit within us, Christians can live in a relationship with Him and reflect Him accurately to others. I will say more about this in the following chapters. For now, the Bible should be less complicated for practical use in your life. If not, here is a summary of the entire Bible to think about: *The Old and New Testaments point to Jesus so that we can know Him.*

Viewing the Bible this way has helped me be more focused on why I am on this earth. Simplicity is needed and welcomed in our lives.

SIMPLIFY YOUR LIFE

Answer the following questions for yourself:

- Where do you get the information from for how you believe you should live your life?
- Do you believe that the sacrifice of Jesus on the cross was acceptable to forgive sinners forever?
- Are you living the way you claim you should be living?
- What is keeping you from living how you should be living right now?
- What is one thing you can change about the way you behave (think, feel, or act)?

Father, help me to live a life worthy of Your calling for me. Show me those thoughts that I need to turn from. Give me the ability to be self-controlled in my feelings and to be in line with how You feel about things. Lord Jesus, guide me by Your Spirit to do what is right. Give clarity to Your people to pursue Your will through full submission to Your good purposes. Help me to make You known to others.

DEVELOPING A DISCIPLINED MIND TO LIVE A DISCIPLINED LIFE

Instilling an attitude of gratitude
Going to God in prayer
Maintaining a continual
posture toward God

STeWaRDSHIP

- The Value of **S**implicity
- **The Value of Thankfulness**
- The Value of **W**isdom
- The Value of **R**epentance
- The Value of **D**iscernment
- The Value of **S**incerity
- The Value of **H**umility
- The Value of **I**nfluence
- The Value of **P**erseverance

THANKFULNESS

An attitude of gratitude

Give thanks to the LORD, for He is good;
His mercy endures forever.

—Psalm 118:1

In 2018, a trusted guide walked me through a process to bring clarity to what is most important to me. The process might appear to some as complex, but it is designed to find simplicity. What intrigued me most from the process was seeing a timeline of my life and God's involvement every step of the way. Here's what I learned: My heavenly Father has been faithful to never give up on me.

Every time I have chosen my path in life, He has let me experience pain that results from the consequences of sin. He has also never allowed me to receive the full effects of my selfishness. He has been a Father waiting patiently for His son to come to his senses and has welcomed me back despite my feelings of unworthiness and shame. How can I ever give enough thanks for His mercy and His grace?

Stewardship's second component is for the natural response when we experience forgiveness of our sin and come to know Jesus, which is *thankfulness.* Thankful people are happier people. Even when things are difficult, God's will for us is to give thanks (1 Thessalonians 5:16–18). Is that even possible?

Before you end up dealing with circumstances that you believe might make it a challenge to be thankful, you can train to stay mission-focused when the time comes. We read in the Bible to give thanks to the Lord because of what God has done in history.

The history of God revealing Himself to humankind through the offspring of Abraham, Isaac, and Jacob gives us many reasons to be thankful. To be precise, God revealed His plan to redeem fallen humankind immediately following the first break in fellowship due to human unfaithfulness in the garden. The Creator Himself made a promise that the offspring of the woman would strike the head of the serpent. The unfolding of that promise through the Old Testament provides a rich history of God's faithfulness no matter how hard people have tried to mess it up. God's promises continue to be trustworthy, which He has proved by the giving of His Spirit until He returns.

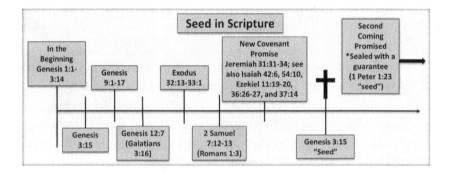

GOD'S FAITHFULNESS IN HISTORY

A king wrote exhaustively three thousand years ago to instill an attitude of gratitude in you and me. His words ring through the centuries and generations. Using poetry and transparency, David wrote so we could relate to his human experience. After examining everything David wrote, we might accurately summarize his words with this statement: "Give thanks to the LORD, for He is good; His covenant faithfulness is forever."

Biblical history gives us a road map of God's goodness and faithfulness in creation. The God of existence is good 100 percent of the time. His loyalty to pursue harmonious relationships with us never waivers. Give thanks to the LORD, for He is good. His *love* endures forever.

The Greek word ἔλεος (*elios*) translated from the Hebrew word חֶסֶד (*chesed*) came to be translated as "mercy." God's love demonstrates that He is merciful toward sinful humanity. However, the Hebrew word carried the picture of an intimate relationship. He never sins. We do. It is because of God's faithfulness to His covenant promises that we are here.

The LORD God promised that the *Seed* of the woman would strike the head of the serpent as the serpent would strike His heel. That Seed is Jesus Christ. He made promises, and He always keeps His promises. He is coming again to fix the broken world. In the meantime, we have God's faithful track record to draw on when times get tough.

Remembering what God has done helps us to maintain an attitude of gratitude. We could list many other reasons, but Scripture gives some options that we cannot forget regardless of our circumstances. The book of Psalms provides reasons to give thanks to God. To honor the previously covered value of simplicity, we will look at three primary reasons to give thanks:

1) **God created us—Creation**
2) **God saved us—Salvation**
3) **God sustains us physically—Eternity**

God has called us to have disciplined minds, and that begins with thankfulness toward God. The following three sections are not exhaustive but provide some anchors in our thoughts to be thankful.

CREATION

> **REASONS TO ALWAYS GIVE THANKS**
> 1) **God created us—*Creation***
> 2) God saved us—*Salvation*
> 3) God sustains us physically—*Eternity*

One of my favorite activities is getting outside with a small group to enjoy nature. Each of us has experienced awe in observing the beauty of God's creation.

Have you ever stood at the rim of the Grand Canyon, gazing across miles of ripped open terrain? We are but specks on the face of the earth. I remember hiking up to a peak in the Rocky Mountains with a friend and being amazed at how small we were in the grand scheme of things. It reminded me of sitting on the side of a mountain in Afghanistan many years earlier, suffering in the cold of winter, overlooking a similar view. On this hike with my friend in the Rockies, I was overjoyed as we enjoyed the steep mountainside views. At about thirteen thousand feet above sea level, several mountain lakes were visible hiding in the Rocky Mountains that sit unseen by hikers a few thousand feet below. My only response was to give thanks to God for allowing me the opportunity to be alive and to experience the beauty of His creation.

We have endless reason to give thanks to God for the life He has given us. It is in appreciating the genius of His creation and our existence that we can first begin to proclaim His greatness to the world around us with a thankful heart. The book of Psalms is rich with this truth.

At the pinnacle of God's creation is humankind. As we read in Genesis, God made human man and woman in His image and His likeness. Male and female, He created them. From the beginning, we were made with some component of God's image and attributes within us. The rebellion of humankind did something to distort that image. In Christ, however, God's likeness is restored in the redeemed person through His Spirit working within us. So God created us with something special in contrast to all other creatures, even spiritual beings. He cares for the sparrow, but He considers us much more valuable than any other creature. The fact that we exist is a reason to be thankful.

SALVATION

> **REASONS TO ALWAYS GIVE THANKS**
> 1) God created us—*Creation*
> 2) **God saved us—*Salvation***
> 3) God sustains us physically—*Eternity*

Moving from thankfulness for the gift of life leads to the following reason to give thanks to God: His salvation. While I was dead in my sin and not seeking God, He began getting my attention. He gave me the ability to hear His message of love for me that was demonstrated by the greatest act of humility there ever has been and ever will be.

During a chapel service at Oak Hills Christian College in Bemidji, Minnesota, a fellow student placed a hand on my shoulder because he could see I was in tears while everyone else was singing. When he asked me if everything was all right, my response was that God is so good. God's forgiveness changed me forever. Tears of joy over God's mercy to forgive and His grace to freely give eternal life with Him are natural responses for the redeemed in Christ.

At the fall in the garden, humankind was separated from God due to His holiness and our sinfulness. Yet, He makes peace with us when He would have been entirely just to wipe us out with no memory of us ever existing. In His great mercy, He forgives us of the consequences we all deserve, and in His great love, He gives us something we could never earn.

We were dead in our sins (intentional and unintentional), and the only way God has saved us is through the gift He gives us. If you are unsure about God's true gift, stop everything for a moment and read Luke 11:1–13. He saves us despite the terrible ways we hurt one another, and even though we put anything and everything, including ourselves, above Him. His gift of salvation while we were His enemies is a reason to be eternally thankful.

ETERNITY

REASONS TO ALWAYS GIVE THANKS
1) God created us – *Creation*
2) God saved us – *Salvation*
3) **God sustains us physically—*Eternity***

Getting stoned to death by an angry mob does not seem like a pleasant experience. Telling people that you know Jesus can cause you to be murdered in public. It has happened throughout the world for two thousand years and is still happening. After Jesus hung on the cross, praying for God the Father to forgive the crowd of hate-filled people responsible for putting Him there, it did not take long for one of His followers to be executed.

The mob sentenced Stephen to death on the spot for telling them that Jesus is the Christ and that He is alive. At that moment, Stephen prayed for his murderers to be forgiven (Acts 7). The reality of spending eternity with God allowed Stephen to have total peace while rocks were smashing his skull in. Wow.

The third primary reason we can be thankful to God any time of day or night, regardless of circumstances, is that we will physically be present with the Lord with human bodies that are eternal.

Being united with God by His Spirit through Christ, we share in eternal fellowship with our heavenly Father. The more time we spend with Him, the more we become like Him. We know Him. His Spirit is in us and guarantees our eternal gift. Just as Jesus was raised from the dead physically, we too will be given physical bodies that will never again experience pain or suffering, nor the effects of sin or death.[1]

[1.] In Scripture, 1 Corinthians 15 is a famous passage regarding our physical bodies and is often compared with John 20, where the reader can see that Jesus had a

Simply put, we will be in fellowship with God and His people forever, which is the hope we have in Christ. There are no circumstances where this is not a reason to give thanks for the rest of our earthly lives.

As tensions grow and evil humankind goes from bad to worse, we can stand firm, giving thanks to the God of our eternal inheritance. Our hope in Christ is that we have eternity with God to experience only joyful, peaceful, harmonious relationships forever.

INSTILLING AN ATTITUDE OF GRATITUDE

Give thanks to the LORD, for He is good.
His love endures forever!

What about your life are you thankful for?

God's faithfulness in biblical history shows us why we can be thankful. That is a gift He's given us in Scripture. Three other things God's people can all be thankful for have been addressed in this section:

1) The reality of creation—our lives
2) God's mercy and grace—our salvation
3) Our eternal bodies and harmonious relationships—our inheritance

What are three things you are thankful for? Here's my list:

1) Eyeballs that work (so far)
2) Hearing that kind of works (despite past choices)
3) Taste buds that really work (since I like everything)

Give thanks to the Lord for what He has done and is doing in your life. *Think on these things!*
Thank you, Lord, for Your infinite goodness and faithfulness.

---

physical, resurrected body.

STeWaRDSHIP

- The Value of **S**implicity
- The Value of **T**hankfulness
- **The Value of Wisdom**
- The Value of **R**epentance
- The Value of **D**iscernment
- The Value of **S**incerity
- The Value of **H**umility
- The Value of **I**nfluence
- The Value of **P**erseverance

WISDOM

Thinking and acting rightly in every circumstance

If any of you lacks wisdom, you should ask God…
—James 1:5

Believing the gospel and responding with thankfulness is natural and easy until difficult times come because of the word. Seeking *wisdom* from God is the next logical step in unpacking stewardship. If it takes all you have, get wisdom.

While in Afghanistan, another sniper team leader I was with received a box of Bibles in the mail from his uncle. In the box were dozens of tiny, camouflaged Bibles sent by the Gideons International. The interesting thing that stood out to me immediately upon grabbing one of these Bibles was that they were so much smaller than other Bibles I had seen. The reason was that they consisted solely of the New Testament, as well as Psalms and Proverbs. The rest of the Old Testament was not there. Psalms and Proverbs are full of wisdom, but why is the rest of the OT missing?

Bear with me as I explain an essential point. When a soldier is preparing for a combat mission and feels drawn to get right with God, it is highly impractical to hand him a Bible and tell him to start in Genesis in an attempt to figure it out. The OT leaves the reader in suspense of the coming of the Messiah.

Newsflash: He did come! We get that information in the New Testament. It makes sense for new believers to start there in personal study of God's Word. Then we can see the genius and divine inspiration of the OT as it points us to the God of creation and of our salvation as we grow in our knowledge and understanding of Scripture.

So those little Bibles are intentional. Proverbs is considered the gold standard for godly wisdom. The Lord has told us what to pursue, and that is wisdom. The book of Psalms gives the reader repeated Old Testament history lessons, as well as language to pray with. We seek God in prayer through the words He's given us. Studying the Bible by beginning with Jesus, then focusing on wisdom and prayer will never cause God's people to be unfruitful.

There are three questions that we can ask every time we read the Bible to grow in the wisdom of God and His word:

1) Who is God?
2) What is my identity in Christ?
3) How should I live?

These questions do not disappoint, making personal devotional time and small group conversation and prayer more focused. You could write an entire book on these questions. The questions naturally lead to additional good questions to ask God. For now, these three are enough.

WHO IS GOD?

In the beginning, God created the heavens and the earth.
—Genesis 1:1

THREE QUESTIONS OF THE BIBLE

1) *Who is God?*
2) *What is my identity in Christ?*
3) *How should I live?*

"Why is God letting this happen?" Being a hospice chaplain has taught me a lot about God. Have you ever been in the room with someone who has days or hours left on this earth and is asking why? What about listening to someone with four kinds of cancer (among other unresolvable issues) who is having a crisis of faith because they believed that they did all the right things to be a good person? Have you ever been asked why God is letting this suffering happen?

A wrong belief about God has always led me to idolatry or worse (if there is anything worse). Either I have ended up worshipping a false god of my imagination who does not exist (and possibly demonic beings), or I have entirely rejected the God of creation and of my salvation (usually without realizing it). Maybe I am the only one guilty of that, but if we want wisdom, we must fear the God of the Bible, submitting to who He is and how we are to approach Him.

Using the question *Who is God* has given me an endless study of Scripture to grow in theology proper, which is the study of what the whole Bible teaches about God Himself. Of course, there are many books written on this topic. The Bible is the legitimate guide in knowing Him and how to know true things about Him. We are changed as we study God's true nature and character.

God spoke galaxies into existence effortlessly. He is present everywhere, at all times, yet beyond the universe as well as time. His knowledge is so perfect that He always does what is right in everything He does.

Another way to think about God when reading is in terms of what He is not, as Eastern thought has done in the past.[2] He is not created, nor is He limited. That is not really how my brain works, but it is somewhat poetic when you explore viewing God this way.

Incredible comfort comes from knowing that the all-powerful God of creation is good. If He were not perfectly good eternally, we would all be in big trouble. While God would be entirely just to leave humankind separated from Himself due to our sin, He has promised to save many. To change His mind about that would be to break a

---

[2.] Apophatic theology is Eastern thought that seeks to approach God or discuss God by saying what God is not rather than to make positive statements about what God is like since God is unknowable in all aspects.

promise or lie, which would mean that He is not good. Oh, but He is good, and He is faithful to keep His word. (Remember?) Everything He does is right and just, and He is bringing perfect and final justice to the world at the second coming of Christ.

Through reading on my own time, I have learned that the God of creation cares deeply for me. He has proven it through messengers, through history, and Christ. God is love. Wisdom pleads with us to know this loving God.

WHAT IS MY IDENTITY IN CHRIST?

> # THREE QUESTIONS OF THE BIBLE
> *1) Who is God?*
> **2) What is my identity in Christ?**
> *3) How should I live?*

"I feel like nothing I do is good enough." At a men's retreat in Colorado, we broke up into small groups of five or six men, and one of the men with a family opened up about his *feelings*. He threw it out there, and you could see his mind racing, considering all the examples of falling short that he had been beating himself up over for Lord knows how long.

One of the older men (probably in his seventies) spoke up, "I think that I probably felt that way every moment of my life until the Lord got hold of my life. Now, I feel that way periodically through-out each day." During a brief moment of silence, every head in the room bobbed up and down in agreement.

How many times have you felt this way about yourself? Get ready for a bombshell because this is an area of struggle we all seem to have. You are not alone.

The older gentleman who spoke up went on, "You know, the Father spoke from heaven at the baptism of Jesus, 'This is My Son, in Whom I am well pleased,' and I have always struggled to believe that God is pleased with me as a son."

That was the arrow. That got me. Based on body language, I believe that those words hit every man's central nervous system in the group.

"*Father,*" the man prayed, "*If only I could remember this one truth every moment of every day, life would look different. You love me and are pleased with me. I believe that, God. Lord, please help my unbelief. Help me to believe each moment of every day that you love me.*"

How many children growing up long to feel worthy of love? How many of those children grow up into adulthood and still feel that way? I am convinced that it is similar for those who come to faith in Christ because too many of His followers struggle with feeling worthy. The apostles consistently note in their writings that we were in a sad state before God saved us. I was dead, a slave to sin. In Christ, the story is different:

> I am writing to you, fathers, because you know Him who has been from the beginning. I am writing to you, young men, because you have overcome the evil one. I have written to you, children, because you know the Father. (1 John 2:13, NASB)

We know Him! Thank you for the reminder, John! We are victorious over the evil one. We know the Father, and we are His children. A loving father loves his children, and performance is never a factor in that unconditional love.

You and I live fuller lives when we accept what God has to say about us as His children through the work of Christ on the cross. Demonic lies hold no power except when we believe them. Has it ever occurred to you that believing lies about yourself leads to sin? We choose to live in fellowship with our heavenly Father and believe what He says about us rather than choosing evil.

My story includes being adopted at age ten, at which time my last name changed from Smith to Crum (*Yes, my name from birth was*

Joseph Smith, and no, I have never been Mormon because they do not teach about Jesus my Lord). More to my point is the fact that I never met my biological father. I believed things about myself at a young age, like I needed to be the best at something. That kind of sounds like how many people think they need to approach God, only to feel overwhelmed by inadequacy.

The lies we believe about ourselves are corrected by God's Word, allowing us to function rather than live under a cloud of lies that tell us we need to overcome through our performance. God chose us. We did not come to be children of God through being good enough. He chose you because He first loved you even while you were still in your sin. What does that change about how you think of yourself?

Observations of the second question from Ephesians 1:3–5 to consider:

- In Christ I am blessed…
- …with every spiritual blessing…
- …in the heavenly places
- I am chosen by God
- I was chosen by God in Jesus
- I was chosen by God in Jesus before the world existed…
  - to be holy
  - to be blameless before God

- I am loved
- I was predetermined to be adopted by God

The last is my favorite: **I am a son of God through Jesus**

Making good observations of the Bible as we read can make a significant impact on how we live. The foundation for sound decision-making begins with knowledge of God's holiness, followed by how He views us. He created us for a purpose. Live purposefully.

God has proven that we are significant. What lies do you believe about yourself that need correcting? Let your Creator define your value and your identity.

HOW SHOULD I LIVE?

THREE QUESTIONS OF THE BIBLE

1) Who is God?
2) What is my identity in Christ?
3) How should I live?

Perhaps the question Christians ask the most is, "What should I do?" This question is most often asking what the will of God is for our lives. The third question I have learned to ask of Scripture is *How should I live?* There are beautiful answers to this question in the Bible. The New Testament gives practical instruction to a broad audience on how we should act as Christians. However, God has given significant freedom to His people. We have a wonderful Creator. He does not dictate everything we must do. Instead, we have great freedom in Christ in how we live.

A professor of mine from a class on stewardship at Denver Seminary wrote a book to help Christians find peace in their decision-making when the Bible seems to be silent on something we are dealing with today. James M. Howard, PhD, is a pastor and the author of *Freedom to Choose: What to Do When the Bible Is Unclear.* Answering the question of how we should live as we read the Bible brings us in alignment with how we claim we should live. For those circumstances that you find no answer through prayer and in your reading of Scripture, I encourage you to pursue decisions that lead to peace from God and consider reading *Freedom to Choose.*

People can quickly become fixated on private interpretations of a text and see little or zero fruit in their lives due to focusing on the wrong details. The Old Testament prophets seem to attract this kind of interpretation from people who read current situations into the text rather than draw out the meaning of the text. This same interpretation of God's Word happens with the New Testament as well, especially regarding conclusions about the second coming of Christ.

Prophecy for us today is this: Jesus is coming! Be ready and be found doing the work He has given, which is to make disciples of every nation, baptizing them in the name of the Father, Son, and Holy Spirit, and teaching them to obey all that He commanded. Well, that about sums it up then, right? Just make disciples of Jesus. Brilliant!

The truth is that we do have the freedom to choose in much of what we do, but (I cannot believe I'm going to say this) we do not have the freedom to pursue sin without consequences. Our mission is clear, but how we go about making disciples is where we must seek wisdom from God in the choices we make.

Asking *How should I live* answers the timeless question about what the will of God is for us: "Rejoice always, pray continually, give thanks in all circumstances; for this is God's will for you in Christ Jesus" (1 Thessalonians 5:16–18, NIV).

I believe that the only way to pursue God's will is through an ongoing, unbroken relationship with our Lord. Be thankful and pray nonstop and in every circumstance. Is this possible through human effort? No! We must submit to His commands and His words of wisdom to us, which involves the next value of *repentance* in our journey of living worthy lives:

> Come, my children, listen to me; I will teach you the fear of the Lord. Whoever of you loves life and desires to see many good days, keep your tongue from evil and your lips from telling lies. Turn from evil and do good; seek peace and pursue it. Psalm 34:11–14, NIV

THINKING AND ACTING RIGHT
IN EVERY CIRCUMSTANCE

Personal Assessment:

Do I believe that God is good and in complete control?

- If No: Am I going to align my thoughts with what God has communicated of Himself in Scripture?
- If Yes: Do I seek moral goodness, and do others see that I believe God is good and in control?

Do I believe what God says about my identity in Christ?

- If No: Write a list of lies I am believing about myself right now. Confess my unbelief in what God has said about me. Pray for the Lord to remove these false beliefs from my life, and to live out of my new identity in Jesus Christ.
- If Yes: Who am I mentoring in the faith to believe what God says about their identity?

I will commit to reading the following New Testament book this month and using the three questions: _____

STeWaRDSHIP

- The Value of **S**implicity
- The Value of **T**hankfulness
- The Value of **W**isdom
- **The Value of Repentance**
- The Value of **D**iscernment
- The Value of **S**incerity
- The Value of **H**umility
- The Value of **I**nfluence
- The Value of **P**erseverance

REPENTANCE

A continual posture toward God in our thoughts and affections

Bear fruit in keeping with repentance.
—Matthew 3:8

"Why do I still have such a struggle with sin?" After trying not to sin and trying to do good, I have found myself exhausted. It has never worked. The first thing that Jesus taught regarding the gospel was *repentance*.

Does it feel like this value should have come earlier in stewardship? Jesus had something in mind when He said to repent, but I have failed to understand it over and over.

Have you ever seen an animal caught in a snare? In reconnaissance, we trained hard for survival. One skill set helpful for survival in the jungle was to set traps for rabbits, pigs, and other potential meals. The animals, when caught, kick and scream and panic as they flop around for several minutes, trying to do everything they can to keep from being captured. Once in a while, the panic and chaos will pay off, and the animal will escape the snare. However, a good snare results in the animal fighting the air until the point of exhaustion, at which time it can do nothing more and has made no progress.

When it comes to getting out of a sin that has captured us, I envision that we stop struggling as we stand before the Conqueror of sin, allowing Him to slide the snare off our leg effortlessly. Then, I hear Him encouraging us to step out and follow Him the rest of the way through the jungle. Jesus knows the way through.

Turn from sin and turn to God. Change your mind. After all, we are all wrong about sin before agreeing with God. That is the message of the Old Testament prophets. The reality for Christians is that we will not think, feel, and act perfectly in this world as God is perfect. (If you have figured out how that is possible, then perhaps you can write a book to help the rest of us who struggle to live out faithful obedience to God 100 percent of the time).

Before chasing after sin, disciples of Jesus Christ must acknowledge that they are empowered by His Spirit to follow Him. The problem, of course, is that we all fail the test. What if there is a moment that you are not obedient? What then? Keeping with repentance seems to be an ongoing process or act, which feels impossible for us because it is. We can end up miserable, overcome by failure. That is why depending on Jesus is the safest, most effective route forward.

HIS WORK OR MINE?

How well-behaved does a person need to be to go to heaven? If you do something terrible, can you lose your salvation? These are common questions people have. Jesus taught a crowd what is required for salvation as these types of questions were brought before Him: "Jesus answered and said to them, 'This is the work of God, that you believe in Him whom He has sent' (John 6:29, NASB).

Humankind has this problem of thinking we need to do something to be good enough for God. He made us good, and Adam caved to the pressure that he needed to do something more. Our responsibility from the beginning is to surrender to His work. He did the hard work, yet we try to save ourselves and fail. Repent and believe the good news! So simple, yet such hard *work* for us.

> **Surrender to His perfect work**

Repentance means that we agree with God that we must be perfect to be accepted by Him in righteousness. Since each of us fails to meet God's standard, we must turn to Jesus in complete submission to His perfect work on our behalf, relying entirely on His righteousness.

THE WAR OF SUBMISSION

A brother in Christ called me a few months after we met. His passion for Jesus was fierce, which is why the call caught me off guard.

With absolute seriousness, he said, "I'm thinking about running. I'm going to run from the Lord, bro." He remained silent on the other end of the phone, waiting for me to say something, maybe to tell him it was a bad idea. *Who says that?*

I considered what he was saying and thinking. In my attempts to pursue a selfish path after Christ, it has not worked out well. The painful ways that God has disciplined me are not something I enjoyed, yet I knew from experience that God let me chase after my desires. I suspected that the Lord would let my friend do the same for a while.

It was as if he expected my question: "How are you going to deal with it when He humbles you?"

He said, "I don't care, bro. He's going to catch me some time, but I'm about to run."

We can only see the outward results of a life changed by Jesus Christ through ongoing fellowship with Him. If we choose to run from our Savior (as we tend to do), we see no fruit and typically get a spanking to learn that our pride hurts others. God will not be mocked and will discipline us rightly to submit to the work He has prepared for us. He chose us to become like His Son. None of us perfectly walks the rest of our earthly life with Him after coming to faith in Christ, so how do we resolve this requirement to remain in Christ?

His Spirit provides the unbroken fellowship we need to produce good fruit. With Christ in us, we have the freedom to choose a relationship with God *rather* than to decide to pursue our sin. The war of submission is real. Evil wins in our lives 100 percent of the time when we rely on our efforts. Therefore, a continual posture of turning to God is the repentance God seeks.

Go and stop sinning.

—Jesus

Unbroken Fellowship

Continually turning our thoughts and affections to God, moment by moment, seeking Him only is the Christian's path forward. Sin is so pervasive in the world and our lives that the instant we are chasing a thought, we can leave the fellowship of God to satisfy our lustful desires. When we continue in our sin, telling God that what He calls sin is not sin, but still believe we can approach Him, we deceive ourselves. Sin is the problem. Jesus is the solution.

Agreeing with God about sin and turning from it is how He has instructed us to approach Him. Are we coming to Him on His terms through repentance and reliance on the blood of Jesus for our reconciliation, or do we wrongfully believe that we can approach Him while holding onto our sin? We must be crucified with Christ. To join Jesus in His resurrection, we must join Him in His death. We have two choices:

1. **Pursue our own will**
2. **Pursue God's will**

There is no third choice, and we cannot choose both. We must put one of these wills for our lives to the death.

The danger in choosing to pursue our selfish, deceptive desires is that we can end up in the belly of a big fish.[3] My friend who told me that he had decided to run from the Lord ended up arrested and

---

[3.] Jonah is not the only rebel humbled by God. Jonah was refusing to share the good news of God with horrible sinners. Is He asking anything different of us?

was facing several years in federal prison. He said that he knew God was bringing him back and admitted his selfishness. God was humbling him. Big time.

Our Maker knows how to discipline us. His discipline leaves us with the desire to live for His will in our lives. The fool says in his heart that he can pursue the first option of our own will. Join me in committing to following the second option of God's will, for too many of us have spent enough time in the past doing what the unsaved do.

> **I MUST CHOOSE ONE:**
> 1) **My will**   2) **God's will**
> **(Choose wisely)**

GOD OR MONEY?

How important is money to you? Money was an important topic for Jesus. We cannot serve both God and money. The kind of repentance that Jesus taught was an ongoing posture toward God, leaving the past's sinful behaviors and living a new life in a relationship with the Lord. All your possessions will be left behind when you leave this world. So, like the rich young man, are your possessions keeping you from following Jesus?[4]

I have had a common thought over the years that if God provides financially for me beyond what I need, I will be extra generous with that money. Historically, the more income I have earned, the more money I spent on things that do not matter, which seems to be true of most people.

The issue is whether I trust God to provide everything I need in this life. Are you storing up for yourself treasures on earth to spend

---

4. Matthew 19:16–26 shows a man unable to view God as more important than worldly wealth. Allegiance to One brings eternal rewards, while the other is deceitful since our lives are but a vapor, and we will leave all possessions behind.

on yourself like a rich fool (Jesus used these words!)[5], or are you using worldly wealth to make friends for yourself so that when it is gone, you will be invited into eternal dwellings?[6] Now we see the condition of our hearts regarding our obedience and whether we must repent. Having a clear conscience in this area can be difficult for me.

If we view the possessions we obtain as belonging to Him, then our decisions change. More important than the balance in our retirement accounts is the need for others to hear the gospel and learn to follow Jesus. Are you investing in the eternal lives of others? We all must repent in this area at one time or another.

Do you find yourself forming arguments against what I have written here to justify your view of money? I found myself doing the same thing because I like the idea of accumulating wealth and having a more comfortable life as a result. The money and possessions you gather for yourself will not go with you when you leave this world. One has to wonder what it would look like for God's people to use possessions for teaching others to follow Jesus. It would be wonderful to see every local church teach God's people to be good stewards of their finances and get excited about using worldly wealth to spread the gospel.

Including God in how we spend or save our money can change the way we view possessions. If we say that giving money and being generous is important to us, our behavior should follow that claim. My pursuit of financial success in the past has led to poor decision-making. Thank God, the Great Physician. It is sinners like me trusting in money rather than God He wants to heal.

When we confess our sins to Him, He is merciful to forgive us our sins and cleanse us of all unrighteousness, then move forward with Him on the mission to make more disciples of our Lord.

[5.] Luke 12:13–21 is the parable of the rich fool. This man stored up wealth for himself without consideration of anyone else. The point is, you cannot take any worldly possessions with you, so use them with other people in mind.

[6.] Luke 16:1–15 is the parable of the shrewd manager. The parable is the only use of the Greek word for *stewardship* we have from Jesus in the New Testament and implies using money to build relationships with eternal impact.

LIVING IN A CONTINUAL POSTURE TOWARD GOD

Answer the following questions for yourself:

- Is there anything that God is prompting you to turn from right now?
- Do you regularly realign your thoughts to come into the obedience of God?
- What can you do to keep in line with what is pleasing to God in your daily walk with Him?

Growing in your awareness of what you are thinking and turning in prayer to God in Christ moment by moment leads to the wholeness of life. It is all about an ongoing relationship with our heavenly Father, His Son Jesus Christ, and His Holy Spirit in us. Repent and believe the good news!

The question for you is this: Are you living in intimate, ongoing relationship with God?

Thank you, Lord, for Your infinite goodness and faithfulness. Help me to remain faithful to You moment by moment, God. Keep me from willfully sinning and hold me close to You throughout each day. Produce good fruit in and through me, Father.

GROWING IN FAVOR WITH GOD AND HUMANKIND

**Guiding others into God's purposes
Genuine love for the Body of Christ
Submission to God**

STeWaRDSHIP

- The Value of **S**implicity
- The Value of **T**hankfulness
- The Value of **W**isdom
- The Value of **R**epentance
- **The Value of Discernment**
- The Value of **S**incerity
- The Value of **H**umility
- The Value of **I**nfluence
- The Value of **P**erseverance

DISCERNMENT

Guiding others into God's purposes

And this is my prayer: that your love may abound
more and more in knowledge and depth of insight,
so that you may be able to discern what is best and
may be pure and blameless for the day of Christ...
—Philippians 1:9–10

*D*iscernment is at the heart of STeWaRDSHIP because it encompasses all aspects of the acronym. Living out all other values well leaves this value on display for others to see. It also happens to land in the middle of the acronym. To the left of discernment are values that focus on our relationship with God as He has communicated Himself to us through Scripture. To the right are values focused on our relationships with others until Jesus returns. Discernment bridges the gap between our love for God and our love for others.

For me, biblical discernment is the ability to guide groups into God's purposes. It is a call to leadership. As you already know, titles are not necessary for leadership. Leadership speaker and best-selling author Mark Sanborn wrote a short book called *You Don't Need a Title to Be a Leader*, which makes this point brilliantly. Do you see yourself as a leader? Well, I have good news for you if you do or if you do not think that leadership has anything to do with you. If you have the Holy Spirit, God created you to guide others into an eternal relationship with Him. That makes everyone in the body of Christ leaders regardless of title.

The simplicity of the gospel of salvation by grace through faith in Jesus Christ results in reconciliation between sinners and a holy God. Thankfulness is the natural response to the gospel. Wisdom comes through fearing and getting to know God more intimately through His word and prayer with Him. Repentance is the only way to partake in God's work in us because it involves a continual posture toward Him.

As our relationship with God moves forward, we come to the place where all of the work He is doing in us begins to reveal what He is doing through us. His image reflects outward as we focus on Him. Discernment is not a philosophical term. Instead, it is the result of living with God.

Lousy theology hurts people. Good theology is good for everyone, as Dr. R. C. Sproul argued before he went to be with the Lord. Sproul taught that everyone is a theologian. Anytime someone has a thought or makes a comment about God, they are engaging in theology.

We are not all called to be teachers in the body of Christ, yet every time we make a statement of fact to someone about God that influences their perception of Him, we are teaching. Rather than never speaking a word about God at the risk of being a poor teacher, we should read responsibly. After all, the goal is for others to know Him as well.

Good theology is good for everyone

SPIRITUAL DISCERNMENT

You probably do not know Daniel, my brother in Christ, but he came out of the Jehovah's Witnesses after reading his Bible. The thing that got him in trouble with the leadership was that he began asking questions about what he read in the Bible compared to what they were telling him to believe. He got in trouble for asking questions about Jesus.

Nobody trained to handle and work with money studies all of the various counterfeit bills to know the authentic bill. Instead, studying genuine bills provides everything one needs to spot counterfeit bills. When you know what is right and proper, anything that is false tends to stand out upon examination. Spending time with God in His word is how we come to know what is true about Him, about us, and those who teach things that are not true of God.

There is an aspect of discernment which involves distinguishing between spirits.[7] In the Old and New Testaments, we read that there are deceptive spirits which can entice people away from God. One of the biggest problems for Christians today is the failure to acknowledge the excessive warnings in the New Testament about false teachers and false prophets. Every single one of these warnings was written two thousand years ago to Christians about people professing to be Christians.

The danger, of course, is that fine-sounding arguments deceive people and discredit the reliability of the Bible. The twisting of God's Word tells us that sin is not as bad as others make it out to be. Before concluding that something or someone is out of line with God, there is great value in asking for clarification to find common ground in Christ. After all, we are to be the peacemakers on earth.

The first few decades after the resurrection of Christ brought us ample evidence that this is a huge problem that can sabotage the mission for Christians to live as we should. The authentic gospel is a message of salvation through faith in the finished work of Jesus on the cross for sin, with the promise of everlasting life with God. Therefore, we ought to be quick to listen to those who say something

---

[7.] The Scripture from 1 Corinthians 12:10 includes distinguishing between spirits as a gift from God in our lives as believers. Not everyone has this gift, and nobody has any spiritual gift at all times in all circumstances. However, like all gifts, this comes through knowing God intimately and remaining in fellowship with Him, allowing Him to operate through us.

that alerts our spiritual antennae. Love covers a multitude of sins, so we should seek to correct false teachings with gentleness.

Every human being is susceptible to believing something about God that is not true, which should cause us to tread carefully in our attitude toward others. (You and I have been wrong about God at some point.) Simultaneously, God has equipped some to be on high alert regarding others' motives making truth claims about Him. We should listen to that alarm when it goes off regarding something that teaches us to follow after other gods rather than to move closer to God.

Is everyone who talks about Jesus Christ as Lord and Savior saved? Jesus says, *"No!"* That is why Jesus explained the parable of the sower (or soils) to His disciples. There is only one soil in that parable that passes the test. Oh, and Judas was with Christ and would be what we refer to as a "Christian" in the way we talk today.

The truth will set us free, and that truth is found in the written Word of God that He has communicated to us through His prophets and apostles. You do not study every counterfeit bill to spot one. Instead, you examine the authentic bill. Read the Bible and learn God's truth from the source.

> The interesting thing about all the warnings about false teachers and prophets in the New Testament is that they are all warnings about people claiming to be "Christians." Not a single alert is about Atheists or Hindus or Muslims. They are all people claiming to be followers of Jesus Christ!
> —Julie Crum (my wife)

SPIRITUAL GROWTH

Watching young children imitate their older siblings can be entertaining and terrifying all at once. You can say the same thing about two young friends who spend night and day together. Have you ever had a friendship that was so in tune that you constantly say the same things, as if you are reading each other's minds? It can be hilarious when two friends are in such harmony that they share the same thoughts. Typically, we see this when people spend a lot of time together. They become like one another. Elderly couples begin to look like one another from the many years spent together.

There are a few things that God gives us to help us grow to be more like Him. The three questions to ask while reading the Bible help us grow in discernment as we align with God's truth and our identity as His people. Here they are again if you need a reminder:

1) Who is God?
2) What is my identity in Christ?
3) How should I live?

Spending time each day with Him in prayer, studying Scripture, and living in obedience to Him as a result is how we grow in our Christian character. It requires our submission, and consistency is critical. Over time, the person we used to be is more distant. We become more like our Savior as we spend time with Him. The first person I ever heard say we must spend time with Jesus was Wayne Cordeiro, my pastor while living in Hawaii.

> **Spiritual growth practices miss the point if the goal is not to spend so much time with God that we become like Him.**

Christ calls His followers to live in a relationship with God and others. We should view the time any of us spends reading the Bible in that light. We spend time with God in His word and in prayer to reflect Him accurately to others in our daily lives. With this perspective, growing in discernment as a personal value means committing to consistent, intentional time with the Lord. Then we will be more impactful in our time with others.

BE PREPARED

Proven character is what is produced through the process of sanctification by God's Spirit in the believer. There is another way to grow, but it might cause you to think that reading the Bible is the better option. As a team leader in reconnaissance, we trained for the worst-case scenario before combat. The plan was to make it home 100 percent of the time. Is that your daily mind-set? Being prepared for the worst-case scenario allows us to function during the most difficult of times. Being intentional to prepare for hard times as a disciple of Jesus Christ has been the most helpful way for me to remain calm in a crisis.

The apostles taught that our growth in Christlikeness comes through a mechanism of suffering.[8] Here is the truth from the New Testament: You and I will suffer just as Christ suffered on our behalf. Suffering might be due to circumstances we are dealing with head-on, or they could be circumstances others are facing. After conversations with people on multiple continents, my conclusion is that, in general, people are suffering.

As we join Christ in His death and resurrection through baptism, we also grow in our anticipation of joining Him in our resurrection bodies through suffering. Therefore, we must, as Peter commands, prepare our minds for action: "Therefore, preparing your minds for action, and being sober-minded, set your hope fully on the grace that will be brought to you at the revelation of Jesus Christ" (1 Peter 1:13, ESV).

Peter wrote those words to Christians who were suffering or would be soon.

Prepare to deal with difficult circumstances. Train your mind to be thankful. Develop the habit of going straight to God in prayer before going to anyone else. Once you turn from sin, keep looking to Jesus and leave the old habits behind. Prepare for difficult times because you will experience them. Oh, and be prepared to come alongside others, pointing to eternity with God in Christ to all who will hear.

---

[8] Romans 5:1–5, James 1:2–12, and 1 Peter 1:3–9 all confirm this reality, which aligns with the parable of the sower (or soils) found in the Synoptic Gospels. God uses suffering to develop new character in us that reflects Him accurately. Therefore, count it joy when you are going through difficult times!

Discernment causes us to listen better, speak that which builds up the body of Christ and demonstrates God's presence in our lives. Train before the battle. Get into the word and alongside the community of Christ. Suffering together is better than going it alone. The authentic gospel teaches us that suffering may very well be God's will for us and that He uses it for a purpose. If you do not believe that, then what is your plan for when you suffer?

GUIDING OTHERS INTO GOD'S PURPOSES

Helping others read through the Bible is an effective way to guide them into God's purposes. SOAP[9] is a method I learned in Hawaii from 2003 to 2006 from my pastor at that time, Wayne Cordeiro. Here is how I use SOAP:

Scripture—Write the verse or passage that stands out to you in your reading.

Observation—Note what stood out to you in the verse or passage, such as the repetition of words, or other notable observations like who is speaking in a passage.

Application—Writing out what we are going to do differently as a result of our observation of a passage is a step in living more in line with what we claim we believe as followers of Christ.

Prayer—Praying for God to do what only He can do to transform us to be more like Him through our observation and application. This should be written out exactly how you pray it. Once through a book, such as Galatians, it is incredible to go back and read through the prayers you have recorded.

Use this method to read through one New Testament book, such as Mathew, Philippians, or 1 John. Use the three questions along the way. I'm certain that your time will be rewarded.

[9.] Wayne Cordeiro, *The Divine Mentor: Growing Your Faith as You Sit at the Feet of the Savior* (Minneapolis: Bethany House Publishers, 2007), 101–111.

STeWaRDSHIP

- The Value of **S**implicity
- The Value of **T**hankfulness
- The Value of **W**isdom
- The Value of **R**epentance
- The Value of **D**iscernment
- **The Value of Sincerity**
- The Value of **H**umility
- The Value of **I**nfluence
- The Value of **P**erseverance

SINCERITY

Genuine love for the body of Christ

Love without a hidden agenda.

—Romans 12:9a

Many people agree that Christians should love others. Fewer acknowledge that most passages in the New Testament regarding love toward others involve those in the body of Christ. We will get to unbelievers after addressing the commands of Jesus to love those inside the faith community. "By this all *people* will know that you are My disciples: if you have love for one another" (John 13:35, NASB).

In the year 2020, I almost lost my mind when a guy said that he was a Christian and did not feel the need to go to "church" to be right with God. The ignorance of that statement may have caused my eye to start twitching. Can we stop letting people get away with the belief that church is anything other than the people who God has indwelt with His Holy Spirit through His death on the cross? The church is not a place.

It is impossible to isolate from the body and demonstrate sincere love intentionally. That is why sharing life with other redeemed saints is a matter of first importance in our relationships. Loving others in the body without a hidden agenda demonstrates our love for God. To exclude His chosen people from our relationships is to reject Him. It is a matter of obedience to God after He saves us: "Since you have purified your souls in obedience to the truth for a sincere love of the brothers *and* sisters, fervently love one another from the heart" (1 Peter 1:22, NASB).

A modern tactic of Christians preaching to other Christians about loving those outside the church has had little impact on the kingdom of God because the love for one another in the body seems absent. We (followers of Christ) will be known by our love for one another (Christians). Jesus said to love those who hate us, but never at the expense of neglecting His children to do it. Come to Jesus, hear His words, and put them into practice: "Why do you call Me Lord, yet don't do what I say?" (Luke 6:46).

> **Obedience to God involves love for His people.**

ALL ALONE

"What does your healthy community look like?" One of the first questions I ask combat veterans when speaking with them is who they live with day to day. Where there is no healthy community, there you are likely to find an unhealthy person.

Encouraging others to get plugged into a community of like-minded people to share life with is no new tactic to help others live more vibrant lives. When someone becomes withdrawn, they can end up with unhealthy thoughts that result in unhealthy behaviors. Because I am wired to include people in activities and life, throwing out a line to others to see how they are doing and encouraging them to get around other people has become routine.

You have likely heard of the bond combat veterans have when they return from war. The relationship formed through suffering together is timeless, and I can testify to the validity of this bond.

After returning to the United States from my fourth year in Afghanistan, I traveled to visit family for Christmas. One of my friends from combat in the army mentioned that there might be a few guys near my family who were in Afghanistan with us back in 2004. Without hesitation, I reached out to one of the guys to plan to get together while in town.

The timing did not work out to meet up with my friend, so several years went by before we finally got together for a few hours. In the army, we saw each other in passing regularly. In combat, we were in the same place simultaneously on more than one occasion where things blew up, and bullets were flying. However, neither of us knew this until we got together for supper one evening in 2018. We are best friends for life (in my mind anyway). That is an example of the power of the bond that comes from combat.

A veteran who struggles with isolation comes out of hibernation when getting around others from shared combat experiences. It is almost as if you can see the lights come on inside someone. Part of it, I think, is because when they get together, combat vets tend to be honest about the struggle.

During His earthly ministry, Jesus taught His disciples that their love for one another as His followers is what would distinguish them from others (John 13:35). We do not read that the bond combat veterans share is stronger than the bond between God's people. Why does it seem in many places that we do not see a distinguishable love for Christians toward one another?

Think back to the combat veteran. Suffering can be a powerful glue that binds people together because of their shared experiences. We see the love God demands of His people toward one another throughout the Bible. As mentioned, suffering plays a crucial role in answering where we will see this among God's people. We can be known for our love toward one another without experiencing hard times. However, the context of the New Testament is most often that of God's people suffering.

> **Suffering can be a powerful glue that bonds people together.**

In the New Testament, there are one hundred occurrences of the Greek word ἀλλήλων (pronounced all-A-lone, which happens to be ironic in how it is pronounced since the meaning counters the idea of living "all alone") translated into English as "one another."[10] The famous usage of this word by Jesus appears in John's gospel, where He commanded His disciples to love one another and stated that this is how we will know His disciples.[11]

Love for God's people is the heart of sincerity from a biblical perspective. A focus on healthy relationships begins in the body of Christ because it is only through Christ that we can have authentic relationships.[12] Loving God's people well pours out into every human relationship and interaction we have. Still, until the body of Christ is known for its love for those inside the faith at the local church level, my primary focus for sincere love remains fixed on followers of Jesus.

Incidentally, if you find yourself in an unhealthy church family, it might be worth inviting people to your home for a deeper level of fellowship. This way, you get to know people and can pray with them outside of the rush of a weekend worship service.

Love One Another

—Jesus

LIFE TOGETHER

Community described in the New Testament carries the idea of spiritual fellowship with Jesus Christ, God the Son (1 Corinthians 1:9), and His disciples. Dietrich Bonhoeffer wrote about the Greek word κοινωνία *(koinonia),* which carries the concept of "life together." The very people we take communion with, proclaiming the Lord's death

---

[10.] ἀλλήλων is the Greek word found a hundred times in the New Testament, which when translated most often means "one another" and is primarily used among the disciples of Jesus Christ.

[11.] John 13:34-35; 15:12, 17 are passages that cite Jesus as stating this strong command and mark of His true disciples.

[12.] Dietrich Bonhoeffer, *The Cost of Discipleship* (New York: Simon & Schuster), 236–47. Bonhoeffer argued for the reality that no human person can have a genuine relationship with God or others without going through Jesus.

until He comes, are the same people with whom we are to have a life together.

Paul, the apostle, even discussed giving financially to other believers by generous disciples of Christ for the brothers and sisters who were suffering greatly in Jerusalem for the name of Jesus (Romans 15:26). Note here that Paul did not stress for Christians to raise a contribution for the poor people of the world, but for the faithful followers of Jesus Christ who were in need. That is worth noting because Paul explicitly told the believers at Corinth that others (those outside the faith of Christ) were drawn to Him through the generosity for suffering Christians they supported (2 Corinthians 9:6–15).

Think about this for a moment: Two thousand years ago, generous Christians giving sacrificially to help suffering Christians caused unbelievers to be drawn into fellowship with God and His people. Sincere love for the body of Christ should be our first mission in the world. Seeking His kingdom and His righteousness first leads to the rest (Matthew 6:33).

Western Christianity has spent massive efforts to attract unbelievers to reach more people for the kingdom of God. The motives *could* be genuine, beyond getting more people in the door to donate to the ministry. However, the people inside have been the most neglected in many cases, so it makes no sense to invite more people. The commission of God to make disciples of Jesus Christ has been overlooked in many cases. The community of believers known for their love naturally attracts others.

The original conversation about veterans and the bond forged through suffering now comes into clear view. Living real life with others brings with it the realities of the broken world. Combat training brings the expectation for suffering, yet many well-trained military members have returned from war rattled to the point of dysfunction. I think the ongoing pain and brokenness caused by everyday events such as divorce, children with cancer and debilitating diseases, and substance abuse can be worse than combat.

Rigorous training prior to combat prepared me to deal with worst-case scenarios. The problem in many of our local churches is that we are not training Christians to deal with the fallen world along-side one another. Vulnerability met with compassion and prayer erad-icates the culture of hiding our sin for fear of rejection. Therefore, a mind-set ready to trust God through the worst of everyday life along-side our brothers and sisters in Christ is needed. Suffering alongside one another is where our relationships are grounded in the love of God.

The reason for many of the New Testament letters was to encourage God's people through suffering, yet today many believe Christians are not supposed to suffer. That is a lie, and if we are going to have genuine relationships, we need to accept that this is combat. You will suffer. I need you in my life because I've spent enough time suffering alone. We need to do life together and invite those outside the faith into the community that loves well.

You will suffer, but we can do it together.

—Jesus

LOVE FOR ALL GOD'S PEOPLE

Jesus prayed for all who would be saved through Him before He went to the cross.[13] He also intercedes eternally because of His divine blood sacrifice for us. Unity of God's people is something we must all pursue. Jesus was passionate about it, so we had better get passionate about it.

Paul, the messenger, sent by Jesus Christ, prayed for Christians all the time. We can see this in almost every letter he wrote to local churches. Paul began by praying for them. More than that, he expressed gratitude to God for their faith in Christ in the opening of several letters he wrote. A study of Paul's prayers in his letters reveals how he truly felt about God's people and how we can pray for others.

---

[13]. John 17 is commonly referred to as "The High Priestly Prayer of Jesus." Christ prayed for us. It is worth reading.

One observation from studying these prayers on behalf of God's people throughout the Mediterranean in the first century is that Paul and those with him gave thanks in prayer because of his recipients' love toward all God's people.[14] Praying for God's people is commendable and the standard we should be striving to surpass for the world to see. Are you praying with others for local churches near you to grow in the knowledge of God's will through all wisdom and understanding the Spirit of God gives as Paul modeled through his writing?

The Sincerity Test: Have I been praying for all God's people across the earth recently? Is my prayer time spent focusing on what God cares about?

Everything in the letters to the first-century churches scattered throughout the Mediterranean tells me that genuine love involves caring deeply for the saints in Christ. As we hear of others' suffering in the faith, we join them in their grief, praying on their behalf to be comforted by God. Denominational differences go out the window when crises and disasters strike. Start praying now for the global body of Christ.

Pray!

—Paul the apostle of Jesus Christ

THE RETURN OF JESUS CHRIST

Concerning the second coming of Christ, God gave this revelation to Paul for the saints to acknowledge:

No one is to deceive you in any way! For *it will not come* unless the apostasy comes first, and the

---

14. See Colossians 1:3–4.

man of lawlessness is revealed, the son of destruction, who opposes and exalts himself above every so-called god or object of worship, so that he takes his seat in the temple of God, displaying himself as being God (2 Thessalonians 2:3–4, NASB).

Some Christians believe God will take them out of the world before suffering. It is impossible to conclude that from responsibly reading the Bible. Right now, our brothers and sisters in Christ are suffering everywhere on earth. If you are more focused on the *rapture* than you are on praying for the church, your faith will likely fail you when trouble comes.

Trouble is coming, so start praying. The hope held out in the gospel is that Christ is returning to put an eternal end to sin and death. However, His people will suffer before that end is to come. Be sober-minded. Pray with a sincere love for faithfulness in Christ for all God's people. Pray for God to send out workers into the harvest. Keep praying until He visibly, physically returns on the clouds.

There is no reward for trading the hope of eternity with God for the hope of escaping suffering and persecution in the name of Jesus. The latter is a false gospel. We will experience suffering, but many Christians seem to confuse suffering with God's wrath. We are not appointed to wrath because Jesus paid the price for us. However, He guarantees us that we will suffer. Lousy theology hurts people.

His return is good news. The return of the Lord will be the end of the pain endured since the rebellion in the garden. We will meet the Lord in the air with all the saints. Until then, we will suffer. Until that day, His patience means salvation for more people, and we all have the job to teach others to obey His instruction to love one another. Encourage one another with these words.

Showing Sincere Love to God's People

Have a plan for being known by your love for one another:

- Host supper for other families in your local church regularly.
- Meet with others in your church family to pray with and for one another.
- Find a small group of trusted, faithful followers of Christ, and be transparent with one another, praying for one another to walk in a manner worthy of your calling.
- Hold a prayer night monthly for God's people to come together and to pray in community. Pray for the body of Christ across the planet. Many of our brothers and sisters are suffering because of the name of Jesus.
- Invite other families to join your family for a weekend retreat with some Scripture, prayer, and a feast in praise and worship of God (see Deuteronomy 14 on Tithes).

Sincere love for God's people is just the beginning of our human relationships. We are called to be lights to the world. Growing in our relationships with God's people will lead to even more relationships as others are drawn into our community through our sincere love for one another.

Father, help us to love one another with sincere love. Give us a heart for Your people. Grow our love for one another.

STeWaRDSHIP

- The Value of **S**implicity
- The Value of **T**hankfulness
- The Value of **W**isdom
- The Value of **R**epentance
- The Value of **D**iscernment
- The Value of **S**incerity
- **The Value of Humility**
- The Value of **I**nfluence
- The Value of **P**erseverance

HUMILITY

Submission to God

Humble yourselves in the presence of
the Lord, and He will exalt you.

—James 4:10

The passage above has been a comfort to me in difficult times. How is your dependence on God today? *What was that? You are doing great in this area.* No matter how much we grow in humility, there is always the danger of becoming prideful about our humility. Honestly, it took the most amount of effort to write this section because not too long ago, I was accused on social media of coming across as "arrogant," and it is already highly intimidating to write anything meaningful about humility. The concept seems simple enough: do not think too highly of yourself. Stay humble before God, among His people, and among all the unsaved people you meet.

Humankind is floating through the cosmos on a rock near a star, and we have zero control of where we are going. We are along for the ride on a planet where we can climb the highest mountains and dive to the deepest depths, yet if we are to assess our reach in the universe, we are pathetic. Our efforts to get ourselves to heaven are like trying to jump across the Grand Canyon. And yet, that is only an image that can give us something to ponder, when the reality is that the distance we must cross by our efforts is infinite and hopeless. Also, there are animals here on earth that can end human life in an instant using their raw power. Oh, and tiny organisms that can kill us without us even knowing it is happening.

Pride comes before the fall. Stay humble.

HUMBLE BEFORE GOD

Therefore humble yourselves under the mighty hand of
God, so that He may exalt you at the proper time.
—1 Peter 5:6 (NASB)

Continuing to walk in sin after receiving forgiveness through my Lord's crucifixion has been the most significant evidence of pride in my life. The beginning of wisdom is the fear of the Lord. It might come as a shock, but the fear of the Lord is to hate evil (Proverbs 8:13)! Wisdom begins with humility. Human beings are evil. We are sinners, so we sin. God alone is good, and He defines what is evil. His definition of evil overrules my definition. Agreeing with God is a step in the right direction.

The Creator of existence spoke galaxies into creation out of nothing. I am not God. You are not God! When was the last time you created a speck of dust out of nothing by your efforts? We do not possess such technology to create one tiny grain of sand without using that which already exists. God is infinite in His power. He made the heavens and earth (the universe and everything spiritual in existence), and He did this *ex-nihilo* (out of nothing). God said let there be life, and it was so.

Not only has God created everything, but He made us as His image-bearers. In His wisdom and power, God created autonomous beings capable of thinking and planning, feeling emotions, and experiencing beauty. Not only did He make us this way, but He made us for intimate relationships for eternity. He sustains us eternally without effort so that we can enjoy Him forever. Looking at ourselves in comparison to God can only lead a rational person to humility. He alone holds the power to create life and to destroy both body and soul. Did you choose yourself to be born? He alone gives life.

Humility acknowledges His teaching that it does not depend on human desire or effort to be saved but on God's mercy (Romans 9:16). Consider that God would be good and loving, just, merciful, and holy even if He chose not to save a single human being.

The right attitude toward our Creator is the launching point for being great in the kingdom of God. He is good. He is just. His justice means that we deserve His wrath for the consequences of sin. And yet, in His great love, He has shown mercy to the worst of sinners, like me. What an amazing God and Savior we have!

GET HUMBLE

HUMBLE BEFORE HIS PEOPLE

In Jesus, we are adopted as God's children, confirmed by His Spirit in us.[15] Now, Paul spoke of adoption that implies an inheritance as a legitimate child of the estate owner. We are co-heirs with Jesus Christ in eternity (Romans 8:17). Every saved person has an inheritance with God in Christ, and He calls us His body, inseparable from one another. Whether we like one another or not is irrelevant because He commands us to love one another. We must remain humble toward one another in the body of Christ. Notice the way Paul explains this to us:

> For by the grace given me I say to every one of you: Do not think of yourself more highly than you ought, but rather think of yourself with sober judgment, in accordance with the faith God has distributed to each of you. For just as each of us has one body with many members, and these members

---

15. Galatians 4:4–7, Ephesians 1:3–14, and Romans 8:14–17 each align with John 14:1–21, promising that God will not leave us as orphans but send His Spirit into each of us in Christ, guaranteeing our eternal salvation and life with Him.

> do not all have the same function, so in Christ we,
> though many, form one body, and each member
> belongs to all the others. (Romans 12:3–5, NIV)

Our humility toward the body of Christ involves using everything God gives us to build up others, as Paul concludes in the following verses.

Not a single one of us can do what God designed us to do without the involvement of God's people in our lives. To believe that we do not need others is prideful and leaves us blind to spiritual truths. It also requires humility to think that God would work through each of us to bring Him glory. It is ungodly and dishonoring to God to believe that you do not have anything to contribute to His people. If you believe that you do not have anything to offer to the work of making disciples of Jesus Christ, then you must work out your salvation with fear and trembling. Either you do not have the Holy Spirit of God through Christ, and you do not belong to Him and remain dead in your sins (Romans 8:9), or He commands you to love His people and make disciples who faithfully follow Him.

Investing in the life of one new person a year who does the same in turn will create more disciples of Jesus Christ in a lifetime than the most gifted evangelist who brings one thousand new converts a day to faith in Christ through exceptional communication skills. A gifted evangelist who brings 365,000 new converts to Christ per year has less impact on the kingdom of God than one committed disciple-maker in a lifetime. Walter A. Henrichsen gave this example in his book, *Disciples Are Made Not Born: Helping Others Grow to Maturity in Christ.*[16] Not surprisingly, this is in line with the parable of the sower (or soils) found in the Synoptic Gospels, where Jesus taught that those who the gospel transforms would produce a large crop.[17] Humility means that we have someone who teaches us to follow Jesus well, and we, in turn, have those we teach to do the same.

---

[16]. Walter A. Henrichsen, *Disciples Are Made Not Born* (Colorado Springs: David C. Cook), 150–53.

[17]. The parable of the sower is found in Matthew 13:1–23, Mark 4:1–20, and Luke 8:4–15.

STAY HUMBLE

A final note among God's people concerning humility: Jesus told His disciples that to be the greatest in heavenly terms, we must become like a child in humility and dependence on God (Matthew 18:1–5). Pride keeps us from that childlike faith and obedience.

HUMBLE BEFORE THOSE OUTSIDE THE FAITH

Christians who talk about the unsaved choosing their sin over God come across as prideful. Amazingly, someone who can claim that only God saves can then turn around and act like they figured out the secret of the universe by their efforts and abilities.

Honestly, I have been guilty of thinking these kinds of thoughts toward those outside the faith and toward other Christians. Having an attitude that we are superior to anyone is warned against in Scripture. There is a misunderstanding of the gospel of salvation through faith for all people who believe. The gospel is what saves. We do not have any unique insight into who will receive it. God's timing in others' lives for salvation has no relationship with our opinion about the eternal destiny of someone who does not currently know Him.

Our attitude toward those outside the Christian faith comes through understanding that while we were sinners, Christ died for us (Romans 5:6–8). We were dead in our sins, and it is because God gave us the gift to know Him that we can claim we are saved. There was a time you and I were not living according to our calling, pursuing only things that lead to death. From birth, sin separated us from Him. We were blind. How is it, then, that we look at the rest of the world and expect them to think rightly about the things of God? That is an odd thing to think, yet we all seem prone to do it.

REMEMBER TO STAY HUMBLE

We do not know who God will call to Himself or when. All we do know is that He called us when we were helpless to save ourselves, and He will call others until He returns. He came to redeem sinners. That is a broad audience on the face of the earth. Therefore, humility tells me to be attentive to those God is calling to Himself, as well as those calling out to Him. It just might be a rescue operation that requires others to carry someone to Jesus.

BECOMING LIKE A LITTLE CHILD TO BECOME THE GREATEST

God opposes the proud but gives grace to the humble (James 4:6, 1 Peter 5:5). Whoever exalts himself or herself will be humbled, and whoever humbles himself or herself will be exalted (Matthew 23:12, Luke 14:11). Pride is what causes us to exalt ourselves over God, choosing to do what He has commanded us not to do.

We must be aware of prideful thoughts that keep us from living as Christ has called us to live.

Humility is the only way:

- Who are you accountable to in your walk with Christ?
- What is the name of one of your mentors in the faith?
- Who are you teaching to follow Jesus well?
- What is an area of pride that keeps you from growing in your walk with Christ?

Father, keep us from thinking too highly of ourselves. Help us to live in humble submission for the interests of others. Give us courage to reach out to others with the gospel.

Living a Worthy Life of Our Calling in Jesus Christ

> **Modeling worthy lives
> for others to imitate
> Always pressing forward
> to reach our goal**

STeWaRDSHIP

- The Value of **Simplicity**
- The Value of **Thankfulness**
- The Value of **Wisdom**
- The Value of **Repentance**
- The Value of **Discernment**
- The Value of **Sincerity**
- The Value of **Humility**
- **The Value of Influence**
- The Value of **Perseverance**

INFLUENCE

Modeling worthy lives for others to imitate

Be imitators of God, therefore, as beloved children…

—Ephesians 5:1

Humility is the pathway to being the greatest in heaven. Jesus modeled this perfectly. Whoever wants to be significant among humankind must be a servant of all. Again, Jesus modeled this perfectly. He taught His disciples this: love one another with the greatest love (John 15:1–17). He came to serve, not to be served.[18] He did not serve to score points with our Father in heaven but show us how we are to live. He gave us an example to follow to *influence* others. In His time on earth, Jesus taught His disciples to let our light shine for others to see, that they may see our good works and glorify our Father in heaven (Matthew 5:16).

How can we influence others using the gifts and abilities that God has given each of us? The question applies to all Christians.

First, I believe that it is helpful to be aware of what is important to us, knowing that God causes us to feel strongly about what is important to Him. For me, this is responsible stewardship of everything He gives. That is important to me, but that might not be the most important thing to others in the body.

Second, we can impact what is important to us by being imitators of God in all that we do. There is a lot of freedom in this because God has prepared good works ahead of time to expand

---

18. Matthew 20:28, Mark 10:45, Luke 22:27, John 13:1–17.

His kingdom throughout time, location, and ethnic groups, that we should walk in them. The God-given desires in others to pursue His kingdom and His righteousness in their walk with Him is something we should openly celebrate in the church. The passion that someone has to be a good steward of God's grace in their life is often a catalyst for others to boldly pursue the passion they have to glorify God as a steward of His grace in their life. Live passionately for Christ!

OUR EXAMPLE TO FOLLOW

Belief is powerful. Do you hold an unwavering certainty that God will faithfully see you through a situation? The history of God's people in the Old Testament is an example for the rest of us. A lack of trust in God led to sin in the wilderness after He delivered His people out of slavery in Egypt. The author of Hebrews warns us not to follow their example of unbelief. The people were vulnerable and forced into a situation of dependence on God. Their lack of trust is contrasted with the faithfulness of Jesus. Then, we get a long list of examples of those in history who believed God at His word.

A lack of trust in God is what leads to a hardening of our hearts. God fulfilled His promise when Jesus came and died for our salvation. Jesus is coming again, and in the meantime, many Christians have suffered. Therefore, we are encouraged to trust God through difficult times. God is faithful, and we can trust Him. He came to give us an example of doing what is right even in the worst circumstances. The example of Jesus has had the most significant influence on human history that there has ever been. He calls us to be imitators of Jesus in our faithfulness to God's will. When God's will for us leads to difficult times, we remember those who are an example of faith in God during the trials and tribulations.

Peter wrote about suffering as much as anything else in his first letter to the church. After years of persecution in Jerusalem, Peter wanted to offer encouragement to followers of Jesus. Living as an example was important to Peter, and he believed that our lives have the power to influence others when we focus on Christ. We are on this earth to make Jesus known, and we will do it by living as Jesus lived: "For you have been called for this purpose, because Christ also suffered for you, leaving you an example, so that you would follow in His steps" (1 Peter 2:21, NASB).

Am I following in the steps of Jesus in my suffering?

Read First Peter some time and note the emphasis on suffering. That guy knew trouble.

Jesus washed His disciples' feet. Our King demonstrated an act of humility by serving those who rightly believed they were unworthy to be served by Him. However, He did this to provide them with an example to follow. Despite Peter's initial hesitation, he allowed His God and King to perform a servant's task. More significant is the fact that Jesus washed the feet of the man who ultimately had Him executed. Later, Jesus willingly went to the cross to demonstrate the greatest act of humility in the universe. God came to us, washed the feet of unworthy men, then allowed other unworthy men to torture Him without cause. Then, while being tortured, He prayed for their forgiveness. Wow. He came to serve helpless, hopeless, sinful human beings like you and me.

We can serve one another because our God first served us. Taking a position of humility to elevate the person in front of us is the example we have been given to follow. It is authentic leadership. God calls us to imitate Jesus, and we are all called to apply this mindset to our everyday lives in our relationships with one another as the peak performance of anything we can do.

For you have been called for this purpose, because
Christ also suffered for you, leaving you an example,
so that you would follow in His steps.
—1 Peter 2:21 (NASB)

GLORY DAYS

Getting a group of military veterans who served together in the same place inevitably leads to a trip down memory lane. Guys talk about their time in the military as the best of their lives, despite the misery endured. For many, it was the best time of their lives. For example, I miss the free helicopter rides to get to work, even though no part of me misses staying awake for days on end.

What comes to mind when you hear the phrase "Back in his glory days"? For some (myself included), Bo Jackson comes to mind immediately. His dominant athletic ability before being injured seemed to make him unstoppable at times on the baseball diamond and the football field. We often think about people and the word *glory* in that way. We think of stellar performance. That is a short window for most athletes, but injury shortened Bo Jackson's window. Still, he is the man I think of as providing a legendary performance in the world of athletics.

There is a hall of fame for athletes of most professional sports in America. There are highlight reels of Michael Jordan winning MVP awards, all-star games, slam dunk contests, Defensive Player of the Year awards, and championship titles. The number 23 is on display in stadiums, on walls, and by fans of the man who could fly. We are stuck thinking about His glory days when he made other professional basketball players look like amateurs in comparison. The stellar performance that Paul wrote about two-thousand years ago was when Jesus Christ, the Creator of the universe, humbly became human and humbly went to the cross of crucifixion to save sinners.

The humility of God to demonstrate love in such a radical way caused Paul to go on to not only boast of eternity with God because of Christ's suffering, but Paul found it pleasing to *glory* in his suffering for the name of Jesus. Paul, like Jesus, set his focus on the cross and everything that the crucifixion of our Lord implies for us. Paul looked at the cross to see what was beyond it.

Paul followed Jesus Christ, and he urged others to follow his example. You will benefit if you stop listening to people who never tell you the truth about suffering and God's plan. Paul considered it a privilege to suffer for the name of Jesus, and he encouraged us to hold the same attitude. In case we are not convinced, Peter seals the deal on our perspective regarding suffering and points to Jesus as our example:

> Therefore, since Christ suffered in His body, arm yourselves also with the same attitude, because whoever suffers in the body is done with sin. As a result, they do not live the rest of their earthly lives for evil human desires, but rather for the will of God. (1 Peter 4:1–2, NIV)

The will of God from before creation was our salvation through the atoning sacrifice of Jesus Christ to unite us with God eternally. The will of God was for the execution of Jesus. Isaiah quotes God as saying that it pleased Him to bruise Him, referring to Christ (see Isaiah 53:10). His will for nearly all His apostles was execution. The meaning of what it truly means to be blessed by God is to know Him more, which often comes through suffering. Do you accept that truth, or do you need more convincing?

Suffer well, Christian soldier. That is what Jesus did.

But God forbid that I should glory, save in the cross of our Lord Jesus Christ, by whom the world is crucified unto me, and I unto the world.
—Galatians 6:14 (KJV)

SELF-CONTROL

"He seems like a crook." That was it; the most upset I ever saw my grandpa get in my entire life. I was about sixteen years old.

"Oh well," he said as he sat in his chair, picked up his Bible, and started to read and pray, moving on with his life.

The neighbor had come over one day claiming that Grandpa Murl needed to pay him something like ten thousand dollars for destroying his property. A branch from a tree in my grandpa's yard fell and knocked over a stack of about forty bricks on the side of the man's house. The tree branch knocked over a pile of red bricks without any cement and no discernable purpose. My grandpa's neighbor said that he was responsible for destroying the man's property and would sue him if he did not pay. My dad spoke with the neighbor, and I do not think he got one penny in the long run after a sober conversation about bricks.

Murl was about ninety years old at the time. He facilitated home-based fellowship in his house for many decades with a humble group of faithful disciples of Jesus Christ who make no claims to denominations or titles. My grandpa loved the Lord. I had the privilege to live with him for a few months when I was a teenager and observed a living example to follow. *Humble* is an accurate word for Murl, but self-controlled is what comes to mind. My grandpa was self-controlled.

Thank God for an example in my life to observe. Regardless of what we experience in life, a character trait that stands out to others is self-controlled thinking and living. My grandpa was the most sober-minded man I had ever met. Far from being emotionless, he was a man who was quick to hear, slow to speak, and slow to get angry. Jesus modeled self-control perfectly and told His disciples to follow Him.

The most extraordinary teaching in the Bible about being self-controlled that comes to mind is in the pastoral letter to Titus. The emphasis is directed at every Christian from the leadership down to those in society's least desirable positions. To be an example for others to imitate (something we are all called to as Christ's disciples), we must take the responsibility of growing in our response to circumstances in a way that honors the Lord.

> Self-control comes through nonstop prayer.

Although it sounds too simple to many of us, we do this through prayer. Self-control is a manifestation of God's Spirit working in us, which is only observable when we are dependent on Him at the moment. God has given us His Spirit of power, love, and self-control. That is the Spirit of God working in us. Let Him do the work!

WORK

In line with remaining sober in our thinking comes instruction from the apostle to Christians who have the wrong attitude about work. Work is an area of life that can cause many to become frustrated. Knowing that God gave work prior to the fall in Genesis can help our attitude in this area, but the New Testament teaching on work is something we should pay attention to:

> For you yourselves know how you ought to fol-
> low our example…we worked night and day,
> laboring and toiling so that we would not be a
> burden to any of you. We did this…in order to
> offer ourselves as a model for you to imitate. (2
> Thessalonians 3:7–9, NIV)

Paul said some pretty harsh things about work to the Christians in Thessalonica. Check out his statement in the very next verse: "For even when we were with you, we gave you this rule: 'The one who is unwilling to work shall not eat'" (2 Thessalonians 3:10, NIV).

Essentially, if you can work and contribute to society but choose not to, you should not be given food to eat, according to Paul. He and his ministry team led by example. While preaching and teaching, they also worked to earn their food. Be imitators!

A strong work ethic combined with self-controlled thinking and living is attractive to people. God's people should live in such a way as to be attractive to others. The Lord used humble men and women to get my attention with the gospel. They live quiet lives in reverence to the Lord, valuing their relationships, working with their own hands to provide for the needs of others. The apostles and early Christians gave an example that more of us should consider modeling to those around us.

The men and women who have modeled Christ-like character to me remained grounded in the truth that God is in control as they have encountered difficult circumstances along the way. Their submission to the Lord and obedience as His image-bearers led them to become more like Him. God has utilized these humble servants to show me what it means to be self-controlled and to work.

During the writing of this book, I had a wonderful visit with a friend, Dr. Lowell Busenitz. Lowell is the kind of guy everyone should meet. His decades of work in entrepreneurship are unparalleled by almost everyone on the planet. Lowell Busenitz has caused me to consider how wonderful it would be if every follower of Jesus viewed everyday work as a calling from God.

After retiring (mostly), Dr. Busenitz began writing a book for the body of Christ. His desire is for Christians to see that God is already in their everyday work and view work as a place to experience Him. I am confident that if only one person realizes how important that concept is, it will beautifully impact eternity.

Each time we talk, I am fascinated by the great questions Lowell asks. He seems to get to the root of an issue, which gives better clarity to pray for God to do more than "*something.*" He is passionate about the work God has given us and how we can impact the kingdom of heaven through our vocations. I pray that his passion reaches the body of Christ and is contagious.

INFLUENCING OTHERS BY FOLLOWING JESUS

The following passages are not exhaustive but provide some key concepts to consider for personal application in our lives:

> Then Jesus said to his disciples, "Whoever wants to be My disciple must deny themselves and take up their cross and *follow Me.* (Matthew 16:24, emphasis mine)

> Jesus called them together and said, "You know that the rulers of the Gentiles lord it over them, and their high officials exercise authority over them. Not so with you. Instead, whoever wants to become great among you must be your servant, and whoever wants to be first must be your slave—just as *the Son of Man did not come to be served, but to serve,* and to give His life as a ransom for many." (Matthew 20:25–28, emphasis mine)

> "You call me 'Teacher' and 'Lord,' and rightly so, for that is what I am. Now that I, your Lord and Teacher, have washed your feet, you also should wash one another's feet. I have set you an *example* that you should do as I have done for you. Very truly I tell you, no servant is greater than his master, nor is a messenger greater than the one who sent him." (John 13:13–16, emphasis mine)

> Follow my *example,* as I follow the *example* of Christ. (1 Corinthians 11:1, emphasis mine)

> Follow God's *example,* therefore, as dearly loved children and walk in the way of love, just

as Christ loved us and gave Himself up for us as a fragrant offering and sacrifice to God. (Ephesians 5:1–2, emphasis mine)

Bear with each other and forgive one another if any of you has a grievance against someone. *Forgive as the Lord forgave you.* (Colossians 3:13, emphasis mine)

To this you were called, because Christ suffered for you, leaving you an *example*, that you should follow in His steps. "He committed no sin, and no deceit was found in His mouth." (1 Peter 2:21–22, emphasis mine)

Whoever claims to live in Him must live as Jesus did. (1 John 2:6, emphasis mine)

Anyone who hates a brother or sister is a murderer, and you know that no murderer has eternal life residing in him. *This is how we know what love is: Jesus Christ laid down His life for us. And we ought to lay down our lives for our brothers and sisters.* (1 John 3:15–16, emphasis mine)

Complete the following exercise:

- Name one thing that is keeping you from following the example of Jesus right now.
- Make the choice to submit to God in this area of your life, changing your behavior to be in line with what God is calling you to.
- Confess this to a trusted brother or sister in Christ and pray together for submission to God.
- Repeat as necessary until He calls you home or He returns.

LORD, make us like You. Strip away everything that keeps us from representing You accurately to the world. Give us the strength to follow the example You have given us in service of others and in suffering well.

STeWaRDSHIP

- The Value of **S**implicity
- The Value of **T**hankfulness
- The Value of **W**isdom
- The Value of **R**epentance
- The Value of **D**iscernment
- The Value of **S**incerity
- The Value of **H**umility
- The Value of **I**nfluence
- **The Value of Perseverance**

PERSEVERANCE

Always pressing forward to reach our goal

...rejoicing in hope, persevering in
tribulation, devoted to prayer...
—Romans 12:12

Proper follow through is essential for everything that matters. Athletic coaches teach follow through with things like shooting a basketball, swinging a golf club, firing a rifle, and the same principle applies to our walk with Christ. If we do not stay focused on the final result of our lives—that we will face our Creator—we may become complacent or overwhelmed with the difficulties of this life. That is why the author of Hebrews wrote to fix our eyes on Jesus (Hebrews 12:1–3).

Jesus gave us an example by setting His face to the cross. He followed through despite feeling heightened anxiety just hours before the only time in eternity past and future that there would be a break in perfect fellowship between God the Father and Son and Spirit. Just moments before His betrayal, Jesus was praying, and His sweat became like blood, falling to the ground as He resisted the temptation He was facing (Luke 22:43–44). His focus was on completing the mission to reconcile you and me with Himself no matter the cost. Wow! His focus was on the cross.

Father, forgive us for not passionately pursuing those things which lead others to be reconciled with You. Remove all fear and give us endurance to know You more and to make You known.

BEYOND THE CROSS

Perseverance always has the end in sight. Every marathon begins with the goal of completing the run. The apostles encourage us to keep the end in mind. We look through the cross to eternity with Christ in His glorious kingdom and rule over our lives forever, not just with physical bodies but also in perfect relational harmony.

Long-range precision marksmanship requires the shooter to focus on a scope's crosshairs rather than focusing on the target. The shooter then aligns the crosshairs onto the target. The Christian's target is eternity with our God and Savior, but we can never hit our target without focusing on the cross. Our Creator followed through on His plan because He never took His sights off of the target. The joy set before Jesus that caused Him to endure the cross was not to be elevated to the throne of God. The Son has always been with the Father. Rather, the joy of the Lord is to have brothers and sisters join Him for eternity. The target of Jesus was the cross because by it we have been included in His eternal family. I get to enjoy Him and glorify Him forever because of His perseverance to get to the cross with my name in mind. The least I can do is remember the Lord until He brings me home.

As we look at the cross, we see God's humility. We see His love for us, which extends beyond mercy and forgiving us of sin. The cross shows us the grace of God to unite us with Him and experience all that He has to offer us forever. It is greater than anything we can imagine. Looking beyond the cross means setting our minds on heavenly things. When we are eternity minded, we are focused on our relationship with our Creator. Then, the distractions of the world seem less tempting to pursue or to worry about.

The world grabs our attention. When we give our attention to temptations, we are in danger of getting pulled off track. When we set our affections on temptations, we sin and have a break in our relationship with God. We are unable to live fruitful lives when we are focused on the world. The only answer is to acknowledge and confess our sin to God and turn back to Him. Then, as we continue in an ongoing relationship with Him, we see His good fruit in our lives.

The spiritual reality involves personal beings who oppose God and His people. We have all experienced thoughts that say we are unworthy of love or not good enough. We have an enemy capable of telling us lies. Lies about our identity and worth can keep us from living to our fuller potential. What can we do about these lies? Stay focused on the cross.

The narrow road leads only to the cross. It does not deviate to the left or the right. It is easier to go another way, and we can be tricked into thinking that it would be better to go our own way. This path leads to destruction. God's message of the cross tells a different story. God says, "You are valuable. I love you. There is nothing you have ever done that I have not paid for to show you that I love you. Now, live in a relationship with Me. It is worth it. I promise."

THE TESTING OF OUR FAITH

You can make a piece of steel sharp, but that will never make it a samurai sword. For steel to become a samurai sword, there is a very specific process that it must go through. The steel is placed in an over because extreme heat to refine the metal, removing impurities. After heating the steel to glowing red, it is folded onto itself then pounded on with a hammer. This process strengthens the steel in ways that no other process can replicate.

Finally, the steel is cooled in water to establish a hardening process of the steel. A Master Swordsmith orchestrates the entire process. By the time the Swordsmith finishes the work, the sword has gone through an intense refining and hardening process to become a genuine work of art useful for its intended purpose. The sword is no sharp piece of metal. It is a masterpiece.

The testing of our faith produces proven character within us. Reading and studying Scripture can give us wonderful knowledge about God, who we are in Christ, and inform us how we are to live. It makes us sharp. However, without testing, we can easily be lacking the ability to function with our intended purpose. The testing that James and Peter spoke of in their letters is like the same kind of testing described throughout the Old Testament as refining the sinner's heart. Listen to the psalmist:

> The words of the Lord are pure words; As
> silver tried in a furnace on the earth, refined
> seven times. (Psalm 12:6, NASB)

The final words spoken through the prophets to the nation of Israel more than four hundred years before John the Baptist and Jesus came onto the scene confirm this need for testing:

> "Behold, I am going to send My messen-
> ger, and he will clear the way before Me. And
> the Lord, whom you seek, will suddenly come

to His temple; and the messenger of the covenant, in whom you delight, behold, He is coming," says the Lord of hosts. "But who can endure the day of His coming? And who can stand when He appears? For He is like a refiner's fire and like fullers' soap. He will sit as a smelter and purifier of silver, and He will purify the sons of Levi and refine them like gold and silver, so that they may present to the Lord offerings in righteousness." (Malachi 3:1–3, NASB)

John the Baptist came preaching a baptism of repentance with water. However, he was the messenger to prepare the way for Jesus. John said that Jesus would baptize us with the Holy Spirit and fire.[19] Are you being tested right now? Do you feel like you are in the fire or know someone who is? Peter and Paul agreed with James when he wrote to "count it joy" when facing difficult circumstances (James 1:2–4) because it serves a purpose.[20] Their strong conviction was that suffering for the sake of the gospel was a blessing.

God uses a process to confirm our genuine faith and produce the character He has created us to share with the world based on our unique personalities, abilities, and spiritual gifts. James knew that God's people would face unexpected situations and the opening of his letter starts his readers off on the correct trajectory of thinking. Count it joy when facing difficult circumstances because they lead to proven character, fully dependent on the Lord.

We are being refined and shaped by the Master Swordsmith. He has a purpose for each of us, and He prepared this purpose for us before creating the world. May we submit willingly to the process. Suppose we are struggling while in the fire. May we ask Him to

---

[19.] Matthew 3:11 and Luke 3:16 have this additional baptism of "fire" that Mark left out in his Gospel (see Mark 1:8). The baptism of fire is not speaking in tongues but suffering and being refined to be more like Christ.

[20.] Romans 5:1–5 and 1 Peter 1:6–9 include teachings on rejoicing in our eternal hope in Christ and rejoicing in suffering, because it leads to proven character as God's disciples and strengthens our desire for the second coming of Jesus.

give us divine wisdom to respond to our circumstances appropriately through trust in His goodness and faithfulness, confident that He is saving others through our perseverance. Fix your eyes on Jesus. Pray nonstop. Suffer well, my friend.

Becoming unshakeable in your faith

Trials are a testing of our faith in Christ. Trials prove the genuineness of our faith, proving that we truly are saved and sealed for eternity with God. In the parable of the sower, Jesus taught that times of testing reveal the condition of our faithfulness to Him. As we endure difficult times and find ourselves desiring God more and more, we grow in confidence in His promise to return and end sin and death once and for all time. Eternity with God enjoying Him forever: that is the hope we have in Christ. Therefore, we can be joyful when we are suffering.

Test yourself:

- Think of a time you were tested in your walk with God. Is there still more to learn from that situation to apply to your life?
- What are some ways you can be joyful in times of testing?
- Do you believe God is working out everything you endure for good?
- How will you respond to difficult times in the future?

Lord Jesus, come quickly. Put an end to the suffering of the world caused by sin. The world only seems to be getting worse, not better. Even so, I trust You to help Your people persevere and endure every difficulty until the end.

IDENTIFYING WHAT IS MOST IMPORTANT TO YOU

CREATING A BIBLICAL VALUES LIST

To identify and define the values that are most important to me, I had to think about where I have seen an example of values to get started since I was drawing a blank. The army was the first place I could recall seeing a list of values. The New Testament provides lists for Christians to consider as core values that come to mind. There are a few lists in Scripture that can help determine those things that are most important to you. Peter, for example, taught us to add to our faith the following values, stating that growing in these would cause us to be fruitful:

- Goodness
- Knowledge (of God in an intimate, relational sense)
- Self-control
- Perseverance
- Godliness (holiness or what we might call "Christlikeness")
- Mutual Affection (for the body of Christ)
- Love

Do any of these values make your list?

In Paul's letters, we can easily see values that were important to the apostle. Would Paul or Peter refer to these things as values? Probably not. However, they stressed these things as central to our growth in Jesus Christ. Here are a few values that can be found in Paul's writing:[21]

- Righteousness
- Holiness
- Truth
- Faith (or belief)
- Peace
- Joy
- Patience
- Gentleness
- Kindness

The list of values one could draw out from Scripture could be an entire book on its own yet could be refined to a similar list like this one. Regardless of what list we use or whether we use a list at all to draw from, I encourage you to identify your top personal core values. Establishing a list of top values central to what is most important to us helps us live more purposefully as His saints.

Some people who might scoff at this strategy of Christian discipleship do this without even knowing it. They might say something like, "We should simply follow God's leading for our lives."

God's leading for our lives often is not as clear to us as we would like, and the same skeptics pray to God to reveal what is most important to Him. They pray so that they will walk in obedience to Him. That is values-aligned behavior. It truly is that simple. Our brains benefit from anchored thoughts and concepts to go back to, so we make better decisions, especially when under stress or emotionally blind-sided.

Here is my request of you: Make a list of values for yourself. As you identify and define your values, you will become aware of how your behaviors align with your claims of how you believe you should be living. It follows that as you grow in the various areas of your core

---

[21.] The list here comes from simple observations made from Galatians, Ephesians, and Colossians.

values as a disciple of Jesus Christ, you will become more like Him. The work of the Holy Spirit empowers you to do this more and more.

Something you have experienced or will experience will create a passion for using your gifts, abilities, finances, and time for serving people as though you were serving the Lord Jesus Himself. Therefore, I believe that your core values are given to you by God for the work He has prepared for you to point others to Him with the life He has given you. You are a child of God. People will know you by the love you have for the rest of His children.

> ## Make a list of your top values.

You can start by writing down a list of fifteen to twenty words that you feel summarize what is most important to you as God's servant. Then, refine the list until it is manageable and contains the top values that you will use to align your actual behavior with your desired behavior.

GAINING CLARITY OF YOUR PURPOSE

Answer the following questions for yourself to identify your core values:

- What are your personal core values that you live by?
- When do you feel most energized and full of purpose?
- Why are you on this earth in this place, during this time in human history?
- Who are you motivated to help?
- How are you wired to help others based on your abilities and resources?
- Where do you make the greatest contribution?

Finding answers to these questions might give you a reference point for how to use what God gives you to build up others in the work of helping others to grow in their walk with Christ.

Have you refined your list of values as far as it can go to live out what is most important to you?

Lord, reveal to me why I am on this earth. Give me eyes to see what experiences You have given to shape me for serving others in this life?

STAY FOCUSED

CONCLUSION

Stewardship is one of the most underrated concepts in our walk as followers of Jesus Christ. Every local church will benefit from a conversation about being better stewards of God's grace in their community.

By putting these words in print, you know my position on the matter. Responsible stewardship involves using the gifts and abilities God has given for growing and building His church. We must include Him in our moment-by-moment life. We must abide in Jesus Christ.

The Lord created you for a purpose. He has prepared good work for you to experience in this life. I wrote *Get Focused: How to Abide in Jesus Christ* to help you gain some practical knowledge to apply to your walk with Jesus Christ, allowing you to live more in line with how you claim you should live.

Stewardship has been unpacked, providing a road map to love God and love people. Each stewardship component in my personal values list helps me live with greater integrity (perhaps a value important to you). Here they are one last time:

Core Values for a Worthy Life

STeWaRDSHIP

- The Value of **S**implicity
- The Value of **T**hankfulness
- The Value of **W**isdom
- The Value of **R**epentance
- The Value of **D**iscernment
- The Value of **S**incerity
- The Value of **H**umility
- The Value of **I**nfluence
- The Value of **P**erseverance

While I fail at living these values out perfectly, God has given me everything I need to become more like Him through Jesus Christ.

By identifying and defining the most important values to you as a faithful disciple of Jesus Christ, you will have a simple framework for making better decisions that are glorifying to the Lord. Doing so has been so impactful in my life that every day brings new opportunities to see God's hand in the world around me. There is no doubt that the same can happen for you. Of course, the values you hold most dear now might change over time. As that happens, you can give thanks to the Lord for seeing change and growth as His disciple.

Uncertainty about what to do is not uncommon. Greater peace comes through asking God for understanding and wisdom about decisions. When decisions lead us down a path away from a deeper relationship with our heavenly Father, we make the same mistake as Adam, believing that we must do something to become like the Lord.

Our benefit in Christ is that He is patiently waiting to welcome us back as we turn to Him. Just as the man and his wife experienced consequences of sin, He will allow us to experience the negative effects of our selfish decisions when we pridefully pursue our desires (my self-seeking will).

Remaining in fellowship with Him is the key to seeing good fruit in our lives, which pours over into our relationships with others. A deeper relationship with our brothers and sisters in Christ develops as we consider the interests of others and do life together. People outside the faith end up drawn into our fellowship when they see our community's unparalleled love in Christ. We can share the grace of God that He extended to us with gentleness when we are grounded in an attitude of humility toward God, remembering that while we were dead in our sins, Christ died for us.

The impact we have on others can have eternal consequences. Many people are looking for someone to show them the way to live. You can impact their lives for eternity simply by following Jesus.

One thing that will cause others to take note of your life comes during the storms of suffering. Your self-controlled responses and joyful expectation of the coming of our Lord during difficult times could be the thing that God uses to draw others to Himself. Focus on Jesus. Commit to spending time each day with Him through His word and prayer. Stay in fellowship with His people. Live a worthy life of your calling, using everything He gives to help others know Him as well. Pray for the Lord of the harvest to send out more workers. Pray for me that I would boldly proclaim the gospel of our Lord Jesus Christ, making known the mystery of God's eternal plan of salvation for His people.

Submit to the Lord. Abide in Jesus Christ. Get focused.
Know Him more and more as you make Him known!

PERSONAL GROWTH EXERCISE: SETTING GOALS THAT MATTER

E very time anyone in the business world has asked me to create goals, it has annoyed me because I am an *achiever*, self-motivated to do more continually.

"*Goals?*" Who has time to waste on making goals? Just get it done. Well, just as the most productive people I know in the work of disciple-making spend less time doing more, I am learning to be a better steward of my time, and this is one tool that is helpful for monitoring activity if you need that sort of thing.

Here is your call to action: *Get focused!* Be precise. Do what you say you will do, and do not do what you say you will not do. What are you going to do with all your possessions? Store up treasures in heaven. Make friends for eternity using godly wisdom to direct your finances to places with purpose: "I tell you, use worldly wealth to gain friends for yourselves, so that when it is gone, you will be welcomed into eternal dwellings" (Luke 16:9, NIV).

How are you going to ensure that you make progress in living in line with what you believe? You are going to develop goals that align with your values. However, you are not going to make weak goals, which are vague and flimsy. No! You can use SMART goals because I want to see you live a worthy life of your calling in Christ in your daily life. Throughout my time in seminary, I utilized SMART goals to be intentional about my personal growth in various areas of my life. These will help develop habits of behavior that are in line with your values.

SMART goals are:

- Specific
- Measurable
- Attainable
- Relevant
- Time-Bound

SMART goals do not give anyone motivation. It would help if you motivated yourself to accomplish most things. For everything else, there are cheerleaders and coaches, and sometimes law enforcement, depending on your decision-making.

To do this, we will recognize the feelings of frustration we have and the thought that this is a waste of our time. We will quickly reflect on our core value of *humility, submission to God*, and reframe this exercise as something that will help us follow Christ more closely. Finally, we are going to respond by developing one SMART goal for one of the following core values:

- Thankfulness
- Humility
- Perseverance

Remember that a SMART goal is specific, measurable, attainable, relevant, and time-bound to ensure practical goal setting. Let's give it a try. You do not have to be great at setting goals to get started, but you must get started to be great at setting goals.

The value randomly selected for this exercise:

Thankfulness—an attitude of gratitude

Goal 1: Set an alarm for five times throughout the day (*Between 7:00 a.m. and 9:00 p.m. only!*), and over the next week stop and pray with thanksgiving no matter what I am doing (*the instant it is safe to do so if you cannot pray while doing other daily activities at this point)* when the alarm goes off.

Note: Creation, salvation, and eternity are anchored in my mind to draw on if I cannot think of anything to be thankful for. My expectation for myself is to give joyful thanks every time the alarm goes off.

Follow-up: After one week, write down what you learned from this goal and how it shapes your thinking to be in line with how you claim you should live. Was five prayer times a day realistic? Should I increase or decrease this goal and keep working at it? Refine your goals as needed and continue to grow until the Lord calls you home or He returns. Live worthy of Him.

Reference List

Bonhoeffer, Dietrich. *The Cost of Discipleship*. New York: Simon & Schuster, 1995.

———. *Life Together: The Classic Exploration of Christian Community*. New York: HarperCollins, 1954.

Cordeiro, Wayne. *The Divine Mentor: Growing Your Faith as Your Sit at the Feet of the Savior*. Minneapolis: Bethany House, 2007.

Ewen, Gary, PhD, of *Pathfinder Integration, LLC*. Dr. Gary Ewen is certified by the Paterson Center as a LifePlan™ facilitator and StratOp™ facilitator. To learn more, visit https://pathfinderintegration.com/.

Henrichsen, Walter A. *Disciples Are Made Not Born*. Colorado Springs: David C. Cook, 2002.

Howard, James M., PhD. *Freedom to Choose: What to Do When the Bible Is Unclear*. Maitland: Xulon Press, 2021.

Sanborn, Mark. *You Don't Need a Title to Be a Leader: How Anyone, Anywhere, Can Make a Positive Difference*. 1st ed. New York: Currency, 2006.

Sproul, R. C. *Everyone's a Theologian: An Introduction to Systematic Theology*. Orlando: Reformation Trust Publishing, 2014.

ADDITIONAL RESOURCES

Bible Gateway provides full translations of the Bible in many languages. This is a resource I use almost daily for quickly referencing Scripture: https://www.biblegateway.com/.

Bible Hub provides many translations of Scripture and has a vault of resources to quickly study the Greek and Hebrew passages and words of the Bible: https://biblehub.com/.

The Christian Stewardship Network has a robust training program available online to begin a stewardship ministry in a local church: https://www.christianstewardshipnetwork.com/.

Clowney, Edmund. *The Unfolding Mystery: Discovering Christ in the Old Testament.* 2nd ed. Phillipsburg: P&R Publishing, 2013.

Comfort, Ray. Founder and CEO of Living Waters and bestselling author of more than ninety books. Ray is passionate about evangelism and has helped many Christians share the gospel with others. Resources are available through https://www.livingwaters.com/.

CoreClarity is a consulting firm that utilizes results of Gallup CliftonStrengths to "illuminate the unique value each person brings to your organization to unleash unprecedented improvement in productivity, engagement, collaboration, and results." Learn more by going to https://www.coreclarity.net/about.

The Denver Institute for Faith and Work is an educational nonprofit dedicated to forming men and women to serve God, neighbor, and society through their work. Their contribution to stewardship can be viewed through their website: https://denverinstitute.org/.

Gallup CliftonStrengths offers an assessment that can be taken by going to the following website: https://www.gallup.com/cliftonstrengths/en/253868/popular-cliftonstrengths-assessment-products.aspx

Lennick, Doug, with Jordan, Kathleen, PhD. *Financial Intelligence: How to Make Smart, Values-Based Decisions with Your Money and Your Life.* New York: FPA Press, 2010.

Ligonier Ministries and the teaching fellowship ministry of RC. Sproul provides biblical training around the world. https://www.ligonier.org/.

The Patterson Center in Fort Collins, Colorado, uses a proprietary process to help individuals and organizations create a road map for living out their purpose in this life. To learn more, go to https://patersoncenter.com/.

Ramsey, Dave. Personal finance advisor, radio show host, author, and entrepreneur. Dave Ramsey and his team help people make better financial decisions. Classes for help with financial matters can be found at https://www.daveramsey.com/classes.

Robinson, Bert. President of *Inpowering People*, which helps people and businesses discover their core competencies and build them into strengths to achieve success. Learn more by going to https://www.inpoweringpeople.com/.

Strategic Renewal Intl. is a prayer ministry that provides resources and coaching for a ministry fueled by prayer. Taken on December 24, 2020, from https://www.strategicrenewal.com/about/.

The Theology of Work Project can be reached through their website: https://www.theologyofwork.org/.

Tozer, A. W. *The Attributes of God: A Journey into the Father's Heart.* New edition. Camp Hills: WingSpread Publishers, 2007.

ABOUT THE AUTHOR

Joseph Paul Crum is a follower of Jesus Christ and the senior pastor at Spring Valley Reformed Church in Fulton, IL. With degrees from Oak Hills Christian College (Bemidji, Minnesota), Colorado Christian University (Lakewood, Colorado), and Denver Seminary (Littleton, Colorado), Joe encourages people to pursue God's purposes in their lives.

While starting day 1 of basic training on September 11, 2001, he felt like he was where he needed to be and got focused. During that time, as a sniper team leader, Joe was born new in Christ just before leaving for Afghanistan. After the army, he spent another three years overseas in diplomatic security while transitioning into his new life as a follower of Jesus. It was not an easy transition, with broken relationships along the way.

Today, Joe and his wife, Julie, are focused on the mission to make disciples of Jesus Christ. They are passionate about being responsible stewards of everything God gives to help others know Him more.

CPSIA information can be obtained
at www.ICGtesting.com
Printed in the USA
BVHW031914040322
630700BV00005B/136